CERAMICS WITH MIXED MEDIA

CERAMICS WITH MIXED MEDIA

Joy Bosworth

A & C Black • London

University of Pennsylvania Press • Philadelphia

First published in Great Britain in 2006
A & C Black Publishers Limited
38 Soho Square
London W1D 3HB
www.acblack.com

ISBN-10: 0-7136-6771-0
ISBN-13: 978-0-7136-6771-4

Published simultaneously in the USA by
University of Pennsylvania Press
3905 Spruce Street
Philadelphia, Pennsylvania 19104-4112

ISBN-10: 0-8122-1962-7
ISBN-13: 978-0-8122-1962-3

Copyright © Joy Bosworth 2006

Cover images (front): Ceramic lozenge with silver
leaf, silver lid and waxed cotton tie, by Joy
Bosworth.
Frontispiece: Stemmed cup with patinated silver
leaf by Joy Bosworth, 10cm x 10cm (4 x 4in.).

Typeset in 10 on 12pt Photina
Book design by Susan McIntyre
Cover design by Sutchinda Rangsi Thompson

Printed and bound in China

A&C Black uses paper produced with elemental
chlorine-free pulp, harvested from managed
sustainable forests.

Contents

In memory of our beloved son, Ben, who inspired others
with his courage and determination.

Foreword

The aim of this book is to feature contemporary, individually made artefacts using ceramics with other materials for practical, aesthetic or intellectual reasons. A few examples are the result of a collaboration between two makers with different skills, but most examples are the work of one maker, and in such cases some of the makers have learned new skills in order to progress an idea.

The intention is to show simple techniques in each chapter and to illustrate the ingenuity and imagination of those already working in this area. Those who want to research the use of specific materials in more depth, to combine with their ceramic work, may wish to refer to the Bibliography on p.110 for more detailed specialist information.

Acknowledgements

I was amazed by the diversity and craftsmanship of those makers who are featured and would like to thank them for their generosity in sharing their knowledge, as without them, this book would not exist.

I would also like to thank my son Ben and my husband, Bruce, for his patience and support during the long process of writing, with particular thanks to our son, Dan, who has helped me with the photography. Thanks to Mike Fereday and Jackie Guest for checking through some of the information, and to Yvonne Ogilvie-Hardy and the wider Bosworth family who are always there to help. Thanks to Michael Jones, who first introduced me to clay, and Elaine Hind for encouraging and developing that interest. Thanks also to Marta Donaghey for suggesting the idea of writing the book, and to Linda Lambert and Alison Stace for giving me the opportunity and for helping me bring this book to life.

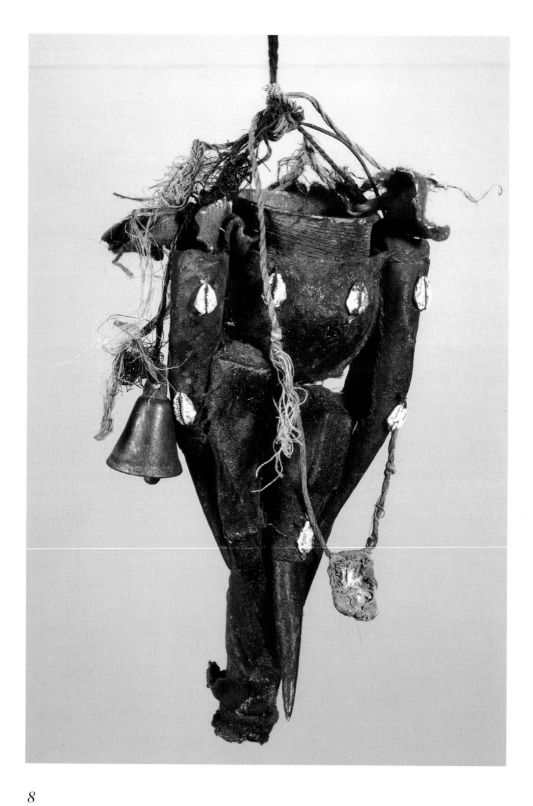

Introduction

Mixed media is a relatively new term. Historically, a string may have been tied to two lugs on a Dorset country pottery flask, becoming a handle; metal staples may have been used to piece together a valued slipware platter; or a metal ring may have been fitted to a prized Persian vase to disguise a broken rim, but these pieces would not have been classed as mixed media.

The latter half of the 20th century saw artists and makers question and reassess their use of materials; it was a time when the categorisation of fine art, sculpture and craft was being broken down. The concept became more important than the media used. The critic Lucy Lippard coined the word 'dematerialisation', which acknowledged this new attitude to the repertoire of materials now considered by makers as possibilities (Scott, 2003).

Art and design education responded to this trend in all sorts of ways. Students were encouraged to develop individual creative identities, freed from the constraints of traditional craft, and were advised to look at the world as a whole and to move away from the classification of art by materials. The term ceramics started to be used instead of pottery as a subject to be studied in universities, polytechnics and colleges. This word-change encouraged a greater

exploration of clay, fire and their usage. Students were urged to explore new technologies and combinations of materials as they became available (Salter, 1996). Later, the universities, polytechnics and colleges began to offer multidisciplinary design and craft courses and modular degrees, with options to work between departments. These developments caused many students to graduate with knowledge and skills in a number of craft materials, including ceramics.

Mixed media is a term that has developed to describe the work of the contemporary makers who have emerged from this creative environment, and this book features those who are combining ceramics with mixed media, both inside and outside the kiln.

Although I do not feel that this is the appropriate place for a historical survey of the use of ceramics with other materials, some examples that have come down to us from the past have interested and inspired me, and may interest others. Very often, historically, when other materials were combined with ceramics, it was for ritual reasons or to give status.

In the Bissagos Islands of Guinea Bissau, the Bijogo people used red felt, which was associated with royalty, sacrifice and fire, to cover pottery ritual vessels. These were further embellished with antelope horns, cowrie shells, elephant hair and bells, 'which may have been used to attract the attention of special powers' (Barley, 1994).

OPPOSITE: **Figure I** Ritual vessel from the Bissagos Islands of Guinea Bissau. (Photo © The Trustees of The British Museum)

9

Figure 2 Ugandan 'ensumbi' vessels of late 19th/ early 20th century, made for royalty by men. (Photo © The Trustees of the British Museum)

In Africa, pottery has always been important for water carrying, storage and cooking, and these timeless African gourd-shaped pots, made by the Ganda people of Uganda for the Royal Court, were elevated by the application of graphite and polish after firing. They were also given status by their ornamental woven pot rings made of vegetable fibre.

The status given to the valued utensils used in the Japanese tea ceremony is documented in an old *Studio Pottery* magazine article about a Japanese tea jar of the late 16th century. It had many protective layers and boxes, which successive owners had provided and which bore the earlier owners' inscriptions. Small – about 6–8cm (2–3in.) high – and brown with an ivory lid, it was given the name *White Dew* because inside the protective coverings lay a poem about dew dropping from the willows that grew near to the tea house in which it was used. These wrappings and protective boxes made the bundle 0.03 cu. m (1 cu. ft) in size, using the skills of paper-makers, weavers, fabric dyers, seamstresses, wood and ivory turners, lacquerers and cord-makers.

White Dew grew in value and its perceived preciousness grew too, as the bundle of protective coverings became larger. It became a ritual to unwrap and reveal this unassuming little brown pot, layer by beautiful layer (Daniel Clark Foundation, 1982).

In his book *A History of World Pottery*, Emmanuel Cooper writes that 'objects made from clay have often taken on the form of things made in other materials' (Cooper, 1988). By the 13th century, the German metalworking industry was well established and, with the growth in the drinking of ales and wines in the 16th century, drinking vessels were made in ceramics to copy those made from silver or pewter. To give status to these less valuable ceramic vessels, some were made with metal embellishments. In the 17th century, John Dwight and the Elers Brothers made tableware in salt-glazed and red unglazed stoneware, sometimes enhanced with silver or gilt metal lids, handles or knobs. Before producing pottery, the Elers Brothers had been silversmiths and probably made the metal elements themselves.

Developments by contemporary makers

It is well documented that Bernard Leach, with knowledge acquired in Japan, was the first to open a studio pottery in England. The production output of small country potteries had been almost brought to an end by a combination of the First World War and the production of industrially made ceramics, but Bernard Leach reversed

Figure 3 Japanese Seto tea jar (Seto ware 1550–1600) with ash and iron glaze and an ivory lid. (Photo © Victoria & Albert Museum)

RIGHT: **Figure 4** Red stoneware slipcast teapot with gilt-metal mounts, by Elers Brothers, Staffordshire, late 17th century. (Photo © Victoria & Albert Museum)

Figure 5 Red earthenware tea set, including teapot with wicker handle, by Lucie Rie, 1936. (Photo © Victoria & Albert Museum)

this trend. His pottery was in St Ives, Cornwall, and he and his apprentices dug and prepared local clay and built kilns, so beginning a new tradition in which studio potters completed all the processes involved in making vessels by hand.

Lucie Rie, a Viennese refugee, opened a studio in Albion Mews, London, in 1939 and, in contrast to Bernard Leach, did not dig her own clay, but bought it and fired her pots in an electric kiln. Unlike Bernard Leach, whose influences were from Japan, Figure 5 shows that Lucie Rie's tea sets were refined and restrained, inspired by the Chinese Yixing tea sets fashionable in Europe at the time.

Rie taught Hans Coper, a Jewish-German refugee, who later made vessels that were seen as sculptural objects. He used steel rods glued into holes in the pointed base of some pots to enable them to balance on square plinths. In the early 1960s he also produced a series of internal soundproofed ceramic bricks and tiles, which held rubber in 'ceramic jaws' to deaden sound (Birks, 1991).

Ruth Duckworth did not use other materials with her ceramic work, but by looking to nature for inspiration was very influential, leading to a whole genre of nonfunctional vessels and sculptural forms inspired by nature, rather than to the pots of ceramic history.

Gillian Lowndes worked as a teacher and maker, and her breadth of vision led her to explore new materials and combinations, which have widened the repertoire of possible materials and techniques for other makers. She was one of the first to challenge preconceptions in ceramics. Her pieces, which include

OPPOSITE: Figure 6 Smoke-fired lidded vessel with shell by Ardine Spitters.

fibreglass dipped in slip, cutlery, bulldog clips, wire and Egyptian paste, are altered by the fire and look like relics or fragments of human experience.

When researching makers while preparing to write this book, it became clear that they had varied reasons for working with mixed media. Some, like Alisdair MacDonell, had worked for many years using found materials as inspiration, both aesthetically and intellectually, and making reference to the history that affects surfaces. He now actually includes the found materials in the finished pieces. Others have developed wonderful surfaces inspired by other materials. Ardine Spitters emulates the subtle colours and smooth surfaces of shells by burnishing, bisque firing and then soaking in layers of copper and other metal sulphates before smoking her vessels in a pit kiln with wood shavings, copper and salt. She incorporates shell fragments to form tiny knobs on lidded vessels.

Margaret O'Rorke, whose light sculptures are now well known, has always been drawn to throwing, and found herself becoming increasingly interested in the translucency of her porcelain vessels. It was a huge leap in her mind when she realised she wanted to cut a hole in a vessel to facilitate the inclusion of electric light, and she was relieved to receive encouragement from Lucy Rie, who had taught her at Camberwell.

The American, Adrian Saxe, through the use of mixed media, is able 'to comment on consumerism, the world of art and our value systems'. He works within the tradition of the vessel but adds tassels, glass knobs and imitation gems to draw attention to the cultural dialogue between art and craft (Bennett, 1997).

Martin Smith contrasts aluminium and copper leaf with highly engineered and polished forms to emphasise the humble nature of terracotta clay, elevating this cheap material into sculpture that questions the 'value' of materials.

Peter Hayes has developed his techniques from the Japanese raku aesthetic, where a broken piece can be rejoined and the join enhanced with gold leaf. He intends his pieces to crack – using clay that he knows will crack during the firing process – so that there is a need for them to be joined. He combines copper and iron oxides and particles in the making process and, when fired, submerges the pieces in salt or fresh water, which alters their surface. He often rejoins using coloured resin, thus allowing the history of the making process to become part of the finished surface.

Steve Harrison works traditionally and is influenced by John Dwight and the Elers Brothers. He capitalises on his many skills with ceramics, metal and wood to make various handles and knobs for his functional ceramics, which are held in place with silver wing nuts and bolts and other silver devices. His exaggerated and sophisticated fastenings give him the opportunity to be individual within a tradition.

Chapter 1
Metal inside the kiln

Gillian Lowndes, in the 1960s, was one of the first to use metal and other materials inside the kiln because she was frustrated by the limitations of working with clay alone. Other potters also now fire with inclusions of metal for aesthetic and intellectual reasons, being intrigued by the effects created by the fire on the metal and on the clay that surrounds it.

When combining clay and metal, it is important to be aware that the clay will contract as it is drying and again when fired, and that there is likely to be some cracking as the metal does not contract. Some makers do not mind, as these cracks form part of the character of the

Figure 7 Susannah Moore: slipcast, smoked bowl with steel pins, fired to 980°C (1796°F), ht: 7.5cm (2.9in.), dia: 10.5cm (4⅛in.).

piece, and use glaze to reinforce, strengthen and hold together the delicate pieces. Some makers carefully select their clay and add paper and/or fibreglass to discourage shrinkage and to strengthen. Others make holes and slits bigger than the metal to be inserted, which shrink onto the metal during drying and firing. Susannah Moore has found that by slipcasting her porcelain forms, which gives an even wall, and by inserting the steel sewing pins she uses when the piece is leatherhard, she can eliminate cracking. She fires bisque in an electric kiln to 980°C (1796°F) and then smoke fires the pieces for several hours.

It is always best to experiment with the clay and the metal used, your methods of making and the kiln in which the work will be fired. Metals have

Figure 8 Tamsyn Trevorrow: spot-welded steel wire armature with paper clay, fired to 980°C (1796°F), 10 × 7cm (3.9 × 2.7in.).

it is designed to take high temperatures being the wire used for kiln elements.

The surface of harder ferrous metals such as iron and steel becomes oxidised and blackened, and Emili Biarnes Raber uses this phenomenon to his advantage in his work, finding that the oxidisation of the metal surface and the shrinkage in the clay forms a solid bond between the two materials within the kiln.

As mentioned in the Introduction, Gillian Lowndes fires metal elements, like bulldog clips, forks and nails, at different temperatures depending on the metal, buried in sand, and then assembles and joins them on after firing. Some finer sheet, wire and stainless steel dressmaking pins can become brittle after firing and Sarah Jones capitalises on this with her delicate porcelain vessels inspired by fabric textures, seams and joining devices.

Nonferrous metals have a lower melting temperature and can become melted or fused with the clay; they will soften and change shape in the kiln. The melting temperatures of some of the softer, nonferrous metals are as follows:

- copper   1080°C   (1976°F)
- brass   900°C   (1652°F)
- gold (*depending* 880°–1000°C
  on the carat)   (1616°–1832°F)
- silver   890°C (1634°F)
- aluminium   660°C (1220°F).

Copper wire and tube can be found at DIY shops quite cheaply, and all metals can be found in sheet, rod and wire form at specialist suppliers. Easily available metal elements, like washers, nails, dressmaking pins and paper clips, can be used as a starting point for experimentation.

different melting temperatures and qualities when fired and the thickness of the sheet, wire or rod will cause the metal to behave differently – and of course the temperature fired to has a huge effect on the finished work. Tamsyn Trevorrow has experimented with the use of a spot-welded 3mm (⅛in.) steel wire armature with paper clay added to its inner surface and bisque fired to 980°C (1796°F). It was then raku fired to about 1000°C (1832°F). The armature oxidises during firing and later rusts when exposed to the air, imitating the qualities seen in flotsam found on Cornish beaches.

Ulrike Mueller has found that it is possible to dip galvanised wire mesh into several layers of porcelain slip which is then fired to 1200°C (2192°F), strengthened with glaze. It holds together well and she is able to make 'wearable art' – hand and shoulder bags – using this process. Kristen Kieffer uses nichrome wire for the clasps on her corset vessels, which does not visibly alter in the kiln after one stoneware soda firing because

Precious metal clay

Precious metal clay is a combination of pure silver, gold or platinum powder, water and an organic binder that behaves like porcelain. When fired, the organic binder burns off, leaving 99.9% pure silver, gold or platinum, which has the original shape and texture but will

Figure 9 Ulrike Mueller: two handbags, galvanised wire mesh with porcelain slip, fired to 1200°C (2192°F).

have shrunk by between 10 and 30% depending on which precious metal clay is used. The precious metal objects are pure enough for hallmarking.

Precious metal clay has a firing range

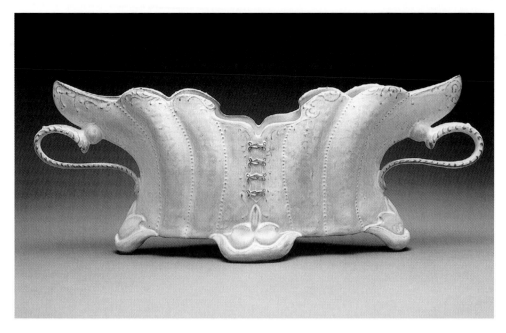

ABOVE **Figure 10** Kristen Kieffer: *Flower Boat Corset*, multiple glazes, fired to cone 10 in a soda kiln, fired to 1300°C (2372°F), l: 42cm (16.5in.), ht: 17.8cm (7in.), dia: 15.3cm (6in.).

BELOW: **Figure 11** Sarah Jones: two vessels with steel pins. (Photo: James Lee)

of around 900°C (1652°F), depending on the type of clay used, with a soak of between ten minutes and two hours. It can be fired several times to repair surfaces and joints or to add new pieces. The skills known to ceramic makers can be used to make metal objects, which can then be combined with ceramic elements to make unusual jewellery or other objects.

Beads made in precious metal clay work well with those made from Egyptian paste, which is a combination of clay, glaze materials and soluble sodium salts, and behaves like putty. When drying, the glaze materials rise to the surface, with the soluble sodium salts producing crystals. The beads are once-fired to 870°C (1598°F/Orton cone 012) and the surface crystals melt, producing the glaze. They can be raku fired, and in such cases the copper present in the glaze may become reduced and colours from yellow through pink to copper-red can appear.

Isabel Denyer makes beautiful chunky

Figure 12 Isabel Denyer: necklace in precious metal clay and Egyptian paste with silver findings. (Photo: Jacqui Hurst)

necklaces, inspired by African jewellery, from precious metal clay, Egyptian paste and silver.

Gillian Lowndes

Gillian Lowndes's ambiguous sculptural objects, like three-dimensional drawings, have been inspired by time spent in Nigeria and refer to mysterious ethno-graphic artefacts made by distant cultures. She looks at the ephemera of contemporary life with a sculptor's eye and, as we have seen, uses cutlery, bulldog clips, tin openers, pliers, stainless steel and nichrome wire inside the kiln. Enjoying the altered and sometimes mangled qualities promoted by the kiln, she aims to render the familiar unfamiliar. In some cases, she has used low-firing Egyptian paste to join together disparate materials within the kiln, but

19

Figure 13 Gillian Lowndes: *Brush Strokes* wall piece (2001), exhibited in Crossing Borders at Sorlandets Kunstmuseum, made from fibreglass matting dipped in porcelain slip, Egyptian paste, wire, bristles and nails, fired to 1220°C (2228°F), 43 × 33 × 23cm (17 × 13 × 9in.). (Photo: Charles Patey)

most often assembles pieces after they have been fired (Fielding, 2000).

Emili Biarnes Raber

Spanish maker Emili Biarnes Raber works with thrown, slab-built and metal elements to make stunning, lustred, sculptural vessels and wall pieces.

He uses iron-rich, red earthenware clay found locally as a background to his iridescent blue, purple, pink and ochre glazes. The darker inflexions of pigment that appear along the edges are caused by the oxides in the clay vaporising in the kiln and affecting the colour of the glazes. The alkaline glazes he has developed mature at between 990° (1814°F) and 1040°C (1904°F), and include metallic salts and oxides such as silver nitrate and bismuth nitrate and copper sulphate. These elements react to the carbon inside the kiln in the heavy reduction atmosphere that occurs during the cooling-down process between 700°–570°C (1292°– 1058°F).

He includes cut and soldered fragments of iron within the pieces (making slits to house them), which adhere during the firing when the surface of the iron oxidises in the kiln. The larger, thicker iron pieces need to be fired with the ceramic parts in both bisque and glaze firings. He is interested in the way both clay and metal react to fire.

Susan O'Byrne

Susan O'Byrne makes large animal and bird forms, displayed in groups, which interact with each other. She first makes nichrome wire armatures, almost like

Figure 14 Emili Biarnes Raber:
In the Evening, 90 × 45cm
(35 × 17in.).

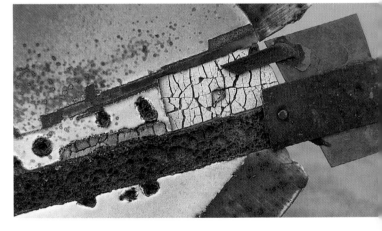

RIGHT: **Figure 15** Emili Biarnes
Raber: *In the Evening* (detail).

line drawings of the animals, then covers these with thin layers of high-firing white clay to which is added molochite, paper and fibreglass. Using paper and fibreglass lessens clay shrinkage during drying and firing, which helps to minimise cracking over the armature and allows additional layers of wet paper clay to be added to dry unfired clay or bisque fired clay. The fibreglass fuses with the clay in the kiln and, along with the molochite, strengthens the clay structure. The shape and position of the animals may change slightly during firing when they are hung from a wire/metal structure. Sometimes the wire inside the body of the animals moves naturally during the firing, creating tensions and suggesting 'shadows' of the creatures' bodies in movement.

ABOVE: **Figure 16** Susan O'Byrne: *Cheetah*, 0.76 × 1.5m (2.5 × 5ft). (Photo: Eric Thorbury)

RIGHT: **Figure 17** Emma Rodgers: *Bull*, clay and floorboard nails. Here she captures the direction in which the tail moves.

Emma Rodgers

Emma Rodgers's sculptures deal with the split second when the intrinsic nature of an animal or human is described during movement. The work 'develops as a dialogue between drawing and expression in clay', and she uses wire and metal fragments protruding from the clay to replicate drawn marks, bone or tendons. She fires to 1140°C (2084°F), which makes the pieces hard enough to survive but porous enough to absorb carbon from the smoke firing. She uses sawdust, straw and magazine pages to give hues from blue to soft greys and browns. Floorboard nails, within the kiln, emphasise horns, bone structure and movement.

Health and safety
Some metals may give off fumes or gases when fired in the kiln so adequate extraction needs to be fitted in the kiln room. Silver nitrate, bismuth nitrate and copper sulphate are hazardous to humans and may cause damage to the environment. Always read the manufacturer's instructions and work in a well-ventilated area, wearing a respirator, goggles and gloves.

23

Chapter 2

Metal outside the kiln

Ceramics can mimic some of the characteristics of metal objects, both in form and surface, and so works well with metal accessories such as handles, knobs and lids. Contemporary makers, working in a more sculptural way, also combine ceramics and metal. Makers who want to incorporate metalwork with their ceramics may wish to learn simple metalwork techniques or may decide to collaborate with a jeweller or metalworker. Here, a few techniques and examples are described to help you begin your exploration.

Lugs, holes and housings

It is important to plan a piece that will incorporate metal because clay shrinks and metal does not. Usually the metal addition is made after the ceramic piece has been glaze fired, but shrinkage of the clay during drying and firing is a consideration when making lugs, holes and housings for handles, and is something that needs to be addressed before proceeding. Clay usually shrinks between 6 and 10% during drying and firing. The manufacturer's catalogue usually gives shrinkage rates for earthenware and stoneware firings, but it is always best to carry out your own tests with your own making and firing techniques. Simply roll out a piece of clay and measure along its length inch or

OPPOSITE: **Figure 18** Joanna Howells: Byzantine vases.

centimetre markings. Check after drying, bisque, earthenware and stoneware firings and you will have evidence of the exact amount of shrinkage at different stages and firing temperatures.

A lug is a small protrusion of clay that is pierced, or a loop of clay that can take a handle. In functional pieces, the strength of the lug needs to be considered as it should be robust enough to withstand use, and the stoneware firing range may be selected for this reason.

Joanna Howells has developed a lug on each of her teapots (see Figure 19) to house a forged iron handle and hold it in the upright position. She has designed her own forged steel handles and learned how to forge herself in order to help with the design process, but now gets a blacksmith to make them as she has neither the equipment nor the time necessary to do it herself. When a teapot is finished, its iron handle is fitted. It is heated with an oxyacetylene blow torch, expanding and softening the metal enough to position it on the teapot, The metal handle contracts into place when the whole piece is quenched in water. A transparent silicone rubber 'washer' softens the ceramic/metal interface.

Her beautiful and functional tableware, made in an Australian porcelain called Southern Ice, is fired to 1300°C (2372°F). She has created a swirling movement in slip, which shows under the glassy transparency of the celadon glaze, to mirror the ripples observed in the shallow sea as the tide goes out.

Holes to receive handles are simple, but need to be large enough to take the handle and far enough away from the rim or lip for strength. The Byzantine vases pictured in Figure 18, made by Joanna Howells, have holes that allow the handles to move freely and rest in the lower position shown in the image.

Casting silver stoppers for faceted bottles using a cuttlefish mould

Simple moulds for silver or lead-free pewter can be made from cuttlefish bones, which can be bought from pet shops. It is a cheap material and easy to cut, but can be used only once if metal is

ABOVE: **Figure 19** Joanna Howells: teapot with forged iron handle, and coffee pot.

RIGHT: **Figure 20** Bridget Drakeford: black and white porcelain teapots, cane handles with silver rings and bone and silver knobs, ht: 22cm (8.6in.). (Photo: Colin Barratt)

Figure 21 Casting a silver stopper. Cuttlefish mould showing 'found' metal object pushed into soft material. A channel is cut for the molten metal. (Photo: Dan Bosworth)

Figure 22 Silver melted in a crucible is poured into cuttlefish mould. (Photo: Dan Bosworth)

Figure 23 The mould is opened showing the cast silver object ready for finishing and polishing. (Photo: Dan Bosworth)

cast direct into it. However, wax models can be made from the mould for use in the lost wax process.

The cuttlefish is cut into two pieces down the middle with a fine piercing saw and rubbed onto emery paper to smooth it. The model is made from any hard object such as wood, perspex, metal or 'found' objects, and because the cuttlefish bone is so soft, the model can be pressed into the middle of the two pieces, half into one piece and half into the other. Make a small channel running from the top of the mould to the model, to allow the silver or lead-free pewter to be poured into the mould. Make two narrow channels to allow fumes to escape as the molten metal is poured. The model is removed and the two pieces

of the mould repositioned and held together with soft wire.

Scrap silver or silver sheet is cut into small pieces and added to a crucible with borax flux. The flame from a jeweller's torch will melt the metal quickly into a molten runny ball. The molten silver is poured into the mould using tongs to hold the crucible, while the torch is used to keep it molten. When hard, the cast lid is removed from the cuttlefish mould before cleaning and polishing.

Steve Harrison makes a strong decorative and functional statement with wing nuts and bolts that he has invested in silver using the lost wax technique. Making the wax models himself allows him to be more in control. Steve makes brass wing nuts and bolts, and makes plaster moulds from them, from

ABOVE **Figure 24** Thrown and faceted bottle with silver stopper. (Photo: Dan Bosworth)

BELOW: **Figure 25** Steve Harrison: salt-glazed bowl with creamware handles.

which the wax models are made. When cast in silver, Steve makes the thread on the wing nuts and bolts by hand, using taps and dies. He uses simple holes in his vessels to accommodate the silver wing nuts and bolts. He makes wheel-thrown, salt-glazed stoneware and creamware, and wanted to be able to combine the two types of ware in one piece. Using silver wing nuts and bolts allows him to do this, thus 'transforming the proportions and relationships between the handle and the vessel' in each piece. He uses engineering skills learned at school in the designing and making of these handles, as it is important to him that his work is functional.

Susannah Moore makes lids with lead-free pewter, which is used because it is suitable for highly detailed castings where good flow properties and a highly polished finish are required. Being lead-free and tin-rich (92%), and because of its low melting point (245°C/473°F), it is especially suited to small studio use.

The moulds are made of RTV-101 silicone rubber, which is primarily used for the casting of low-melt alloys and can cope with temperatures up to 316°C (601°F) when casting white metals. These materials can be bought from a good art or sculptural supplier.

Some basic metalwork forming techniques

Cutting metal sheet

For small cutting jobs, tin snips work well, although they will damage edges, which will therefore need to be filed. If a more hand-wrought look is required then the edge can be hammered, which minimises finishing. For more complex cuts a jeweller's piercing saw should be used.

Figure 26 Susannah Moore: ceramic vessels with pewter stoppers, l: 44cm (17in.). (Photo: Ricki Knight)

Forming

Silver, gold and copper (and to a lesser extent brass and gilding metal) are quite soft and can be bent with the fingers, but for clean, professional bends and changes in direction, it is best to work around a wooden or metal former chosen for the job. A polythene or wooden mallet may be used to assist forming without damaging the surface of the metal. Specialist jeweller's pliers (i.e. round-nose pliers) will help in making specific shapes.

Annealing

During the making process metal becomes work-hardened and may need annealing several times to make it easier to bend, form and manipulate. You will need a jeweller's small gas torch for this, which can be bought from a jeweller's supplier. Annealing is done by heating the piece evenly until it becomes a cherry red all over, when it will have reached its annealing temperature. Once it has been annealed, it is cleaned in a 'pickle' (a solution of one part sulphuric acid to ten parts water).

Silver soldering

This process permanently joins two pieces of metal using flux, solder and heat. It is possible to use this technique on silver, brass, copper and gilding metal. Special gold solder is used for working with gold. Sometimes one project requires a number of soldered joins, and there are several different grades of solder that melt at different temperatures for this purpose. Solder is cut into tiny pieces, or pallions, with tin snips, which are painted with borax flux, being applied to the work with either a borax brush or tweezers.

Borax flux comes in hard white cones, which are rubbed into a dish with small amounts of water. This creates a milky solution that, when painted onto the clean metal about to be joined, will keep the area clean and promote the flow of solder.

Metals to be joined need to be clean, to have borax and solder pallions applied, to be in contact with each other along the part to be joined, and to be equally hot. If any one of these requirements is not met the solder will not flow. Both pieces of metal need to be cherry red and, when two pieces of differing size are to be joined, the larger piece is heated first because it takes longer, and then the torch is played over both pieces until an even heat is achieved. It will be possible to see a bright, shiny flowing line or puddle of solder when it has melted. The work is then cooled under a tap and placed into the pickle to become clean again.

Figure 27 Cutting silver sheet with tin snips. (Photo: Dan Bosworth)

Forming and soldering a silver lid

This section offers a practical description, along with appropriate images, of how a silver lid is formed and soldered.

Make a paper pattern for the top and the collar. Mark onto the sheet metal with a scribe or sharp point. Cut the top to size with tin snips. Gently hammer the edge with a ball plein hammer onto a metal block and smooth with a file. Cut the collar with tin snips, file the edges and bend against the edge of square-nosed pliers so that the join butts together in the middle of one of the sides.

Hold together with iron binding wire. Position upside down, resting on the underside of the flat top. Apply borax flux and pallions of medium solder to all joins.

Heat the work until the solder flows. Quench in water and gently drop into the pickle to clean the silver. To make the

Figure 27a Gently hammer edge with ball-plein hammer.

Figure 27b Bend the collar against the edge of square nosed pliers.

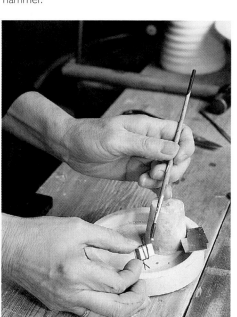

Figure 27c Hold together with iron binding wire. Paint borax flux over pallions of silver solder and the joins and then apply pallions to the collar with the tip of a borax brush.

Figure 27d The lid top and collar are positioned with borax flux and solder pallions. Heat with a torch until the solder flows. (All photos: Dan Bosworth)

Figure 28 Position upside down resting on the underside of the flat top. Apply borax flux and pallions of medium solder to all the joins. Heat the work until the solder flows.

Figure 29 Polish with a jewellers pendant motor and jewellers' rouge. You may prefer to use silver metal polish and a rag but it will take longer.

Figure 30 Finished ceramic lozenge with silver leaf, silver lid and waxed cotton tie. (All photos: Dan Bosworth).

wire lug, bend the wire around round-nose pliers and cut to size. Hold with tweezers and apply borax flux and soft ('easy') solder pallions to each end of silver wire lug. Hold in position over the lid. Heat the lid and then the wire lug, which should join when the solder flows; quench in water and pickle. Polish with a metal cleaner and clean rag or with a jeweller's pendant motor and jeweller's rouge.

Steve Harrison has developed a number of types of handle and knob fittings for mugs and teapots. The handle of the mug in the foreground of Figure 31 is joined with a complex system requiring skill and precision. The handle has, at each end, a clay lug protruding, which fits around similar lugs on the vessel.

Holes in each lug, made while leather-hard, are aligned with those in a silver collar through which silver rivets are

Figure 31 Steve Harrison: pots with various fittings.

RIGHT: **Figure 32** Handle fitment.

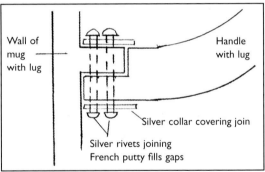

Wall of
mug
with lug

Handle
with lug

Silver collar covering join

Silver rivets joining
French putty fills gaps

threaded to hold the join together. French putty is applied to the components before positioning to cushion and fix the join.

Other decorative uses of metal and ceramic components

Sarah Cilia is a jeweller whose distinctive jewellery combines textured sheets of porcelain with silver and gold. She started to use porcelain because of its potential for mimicking handmade paper. Here is described the making of Sarah Cilia's brooch.

A small plaster mould of the handmade paper is prepared. A thin sheet of porcelain is rolled over the plaster, which takes on the texture of the handmade paper from the mould. The porcelain is fired to 1260°C (2300°F) without glaze. The silver frame on the brooch is made from square-section rod and the filigree detail is made from forged, shaped and soldered elements. The porcelain is held by three forged silver pins, which are soldered then folded back against the porcelain, holding it firmly in place.

Figure 33 Sarah Cilia: brooch forged and soldered, silver and gold with porcelain.

OPPOSITE: **Figure 34** Tony Foard: *Three African Women.*

A number of makers use wire to join multiple small elements into a larger piece or to enhance other pieces. Copper, brass, aluminium and silver wire have good colour and are easy to bend with round-nose pliers. Some use manufactured findings or clamps.

Tony Foard's individually handbuilt African female figures (see Figure 34) are made with white clay, used for its purity, which he fires using the techniques of raku and smoke firing. The tall figures have tin- or silver-plated copper-wire neckpieces or collars that disguise the join, which is fixed with an industrial bonding substance. The neckpieces are slightly patinated with the flame of a torch for decorative effect.

Some more complex silver head-dresses and silver neckpieces (like the one in the middle of the image) are made

by a jeweller friend, Michael Bolton, with whom Foard collaborates.

Inspired by mosque towers in the Sultanate of Oman, the intricately made bone china elements shown in Figure 35 by Elizabeth Smith are fired to 1240°C (2264°F) and assembled with aluminium beading wire to form a window piece.

Ulrike Mueller was first interested in the idea of wearable ceramics, and worked with ceramics and mixed media to make 'pieces of art that could also be worn on special occasions'. First, she made jewellery but found the size involved did not give enough scope so she started working with a series of bags, which developed quickly and with a variety of materials. Figure 36 shows *Sticks Bag – White*, which is made of Limoges porcelain, fired to 1260°C (2300°F) without glaze and then put together with high-

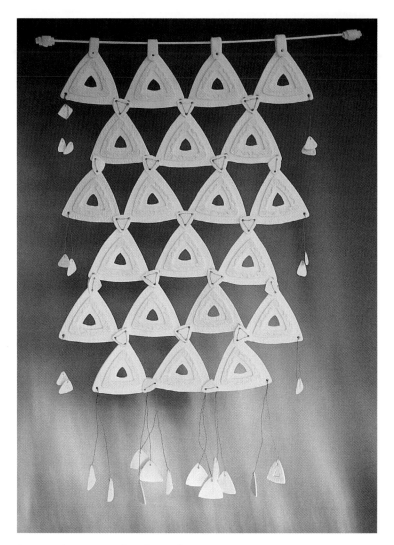

grade stainless steel connected with steel clamps and lined with loden cloth.

Lisa Hammond's hand-thrown, raw-glazed, soda-fired cafetière utilises a manufactured metal plunger. Developing the idea took a great deal of work: she had to source the metal plunger, test the shrinkage of the clay and work out a way of making allowances for any variation in the thrown cylinder of the cafetiere. She created some flexibility by easing out the layer of springy metal gauze that filters the coffee grounds.

Figure 35 Elizabeth Smith: *Anisa.*

Collaboration with small manufacturers

Some makers who wish to make more complex pieces prefer to collaborate with small manufacturers, who may have special equipment and skills.

In the last few years, Jean-Paul Landreau has become interested in making tables in collaboration with a

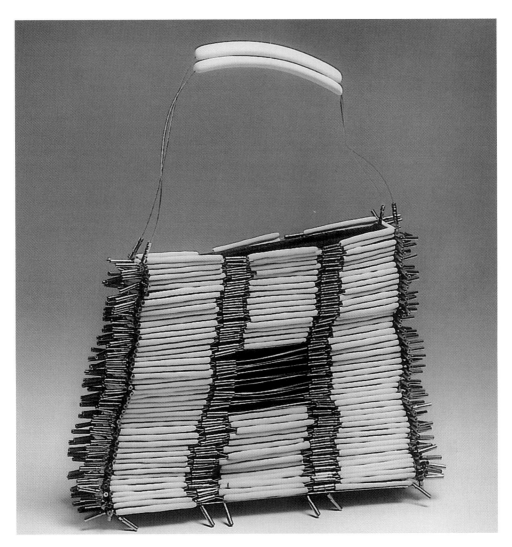

Figure 36 Ulrike Mueller: *Sticks Bag – White.*

metal manufacturer. He feels strongly that the quality of the metalwork should be of a high standard in order to complement the ceramics. It has taken two years of research and development to find the right design, process and manufacturer to produce consistently good quality at the right price.

Though the galvanising process gives metal a good rust-proof surface, it is not suitable for Landreau's tables because it causes distortion in the metalwork and the surface quality is not good enough to receive the matt-black paint. He has found that electroplating with zinc and then powder coating in matt black provides a neat, rust-proof black table that acts as a good foil for his colourful, painterly ceramic tabletops.

His large plates, bowls and tabletops provide a 'canvas' for 'multiple layers of coloured slips and sgraffito, which are influenced by Leger, Cocteau and Braque'. He uses both oxides and body

LEFT: **Figure 37** Jean-Paul Landreau: metal table with painted thrown ceramic top, dia: 50–55cm (19½–21½in.).

BELOW LEFT: **Figure 38** Lisa Hammond: soda-fired cafetière. (Photo: Will Thom)

stains at between 5% and 20% to achieve the palette, which is added to a slip made of ball clay and china clay, sometimes with a small amount of borax frit to help the adhesion of the slip to the clay surface.

He uses a smooth, white earthenware clay glazed and fired to 1160°C (2120°F) in an oxidised electric kiln. For the table-tops he makes a thrown 'tile' of 50–55cm (19½–21½in.) diameter, which is challeng-ing, because he does not want to use grog as it would interfere with the sgraffito design. To prevent warping and crack-ing, he needs to dry very slowly. He also needs to fire slowly, controlling the slow build-up of temperature as well as the cooling of both bisque and glaze firing.

Health and safety
Chemicals may be dangerous and corrosive. Always read the instructions on the manufacturer's label. Wear rubber gloves when working with chemicals; always add the chemicals to water – never vice versa. Make sure you work in a well-ventilated place; store chemicals in a locked, dry, cool place, out of the reach of children. Buy 'safe' pickle where possible – it is less caustic and comes in white crystals that are diluted in water. Pickle needs to be kept in a glass container and works better when warmed in a saucepan of water over heat.

Chapter 3

Mixed media surface treatments

Historically, 'primitive' potters have used different, sometimes secret, concoctions of milk, vegetable oils, beeswax or other substances with burnishing, to seal low-fired pots. Graphite, shoe polish and even cellulose spray paint are used by some to colour pots, but I think the term mixed media is rather tenuous in these cases. This chapter suggests other ways in which you may wish to experiment with mixed media on the surface of ceramic pieces, either melted into the surface in the kiln or applied afterwards as a decorative surface.

Figure 39 Phyllis Dupuy: gold leaf melted into the surface of stoneware glazed vessel, dia: 22cm (8.6in.). (Photo: Susie Ahlburg)

Surfaces created with metal inside the kiln

Metal oxides occurring naturally within a clay body or added to a glaze have traditionally been used to colour ceramics. Today, some potters use actual wire, sheet, metal leaf or foil inside the kiln to enhance the surface of their work.

Nonferrous metals are generally softer than ferrous metals and melt between 660°C (1220°F) and 1080°C (1976°F), affecting the surface of the clay and the glaze around them; however, all metals other than gold will oxidise. Phyllis Dupuy (see figure 39) melts gold leaf into the surface of her finely thrown, turquoise bowls, made in Limoges porcelain. The barium glaze is

fired to 1280°C (2336°F) and then the 22-carat gold leaf is applied to the surface over a layer of lavender oil and pine resin that has been allowed to dry to a tacky surface. The work is fired again to 750°C (1382°F), which allows the gold to melt into the surface of the glaze. At this temperature, it becomes transparent, revealing the overlapping layers of gold. Care must be taken with temperature control because gold leaf vaporises at 785°C (1445°F).

Gwen Bainbridge has experimented with precious metal clay fused onto the surface of slipcast bone china forms. Precious metal clay combines the powder of precious metals with an organic binder that burns away in the kiln. The resulting material is 99.9% silver and can be hallmarked. (Further details can be found in Chapter 1.) Gwen has found that if a slip is made out of the precious metal clay she can add it to the surface of her slipcast bone china forms and, when fired, it forms a beaded, frosted silver surface. Rather than have the silver surface all over the form she sometimes masks off some areas with latex or shellac, and sandblasts to give a raised pattern. The bone china is then fired to 1230°C (2246°F) with a 90-minute soak that drops to cone 8. The precious metal clay slip is applied to the fired piece in layers and left to dry naturally between coats. She then fires the pieces to 1100°C (2012°F), which causes the silver to form tiny beads. The beakers and vases are glazed and re-fired after the silver surface has been fired on. The disadvantage of using silver is that it tarnishes and needs regular cleaning with a soft cloth. A silver polish can be used on more tarnished areas and the pot then needs to be washed to remove the polish.

One recommended supplier is Silver Alchemy (see the 'Suppliers' section at the back of the book).

Tamsyn Trevorrow has experimented with a variety of metal wire at different temperatures and, in Figure 42, she shows the surface achieved by building a 3mm (⅛in.) steel wire and clay structure, which was bisque fired to 980°C (1796°F) and glaze fired to 1260°C (2300°F) with a dry glaze. The wire melted into the piece, imitating the corrosion caused by sea air. Figure 41 shows how 0.5mm (¹⁄₆₄in.) copper wire, which has been bound around the tea bowl, melts at 1260°C (2300°F) producing a green/ black line in the glaze.

Figure 40 Gwen Bainbridge: precious metal clay slip melted onto a surface.

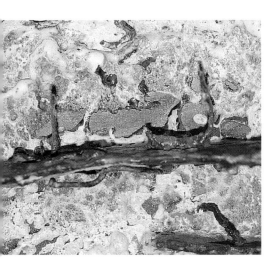

In this detail of the *Child Teaser Jar* (Figure 43) Susannah Moore has contrasted the round, smooth form with a dangerous spiky interior by piercing steel pins through the vessel at the leatherhard stage. When fired, the pins oxidise; over time, they rust as they absorb the moisture in the atmosphere, allowing iron oxide to seep into the surrounding clay.

ABOVE: **Figure 41** Tamsyn Trevorrow: using copper wire at different temperatures.
ABOVE LEFT: **Figure 42** detail of Figure 41.

BELOW: **Figure 43** Susannah Moore: *Child Teaser Jar*.

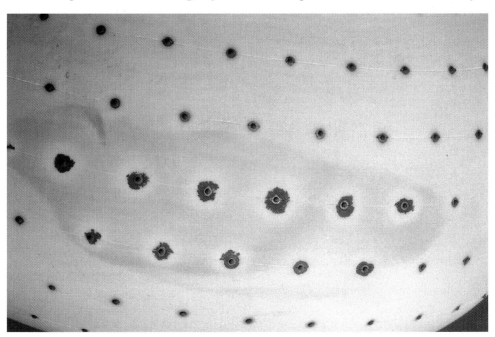

Figure 44 Duncan Ayscough: gold leaf with smoke-fired terra sigillata.

Metal leaf applied after firing

Some potters prefer to use metal leaf on decorative ceramic pieces, instead of commercial ceramic metal lustres, because of its special qualities. Copper, silver, aluminium, gold and Dutch metal leaf can either be bought loose or as transfer metal leaf. Transfer metal leaf is lightly attached to waxed or tissue paper, which makes it easier to pick up and cut, ready for applying. The transfer metal leaf is positioned by holding the over-hanging transfer paper, which will come free when the metal leaf has adhered to the gold size. It should be rubbed with the fingers to ensure that all the metal leaf has adhered. Any excess can be removed with a soft brush. Gaps can be filled with extra pieces of metal leaf, but the character of the cracks that natu-rally occur, as well as the gaps between squares, are used by some makers as

an aesthetic effect.

'Gold size', which has historically been used to prepare the surface, does not tarnish the metal leaf. It can be bought in either water-based or oil-based versions. Water-based size is easier for the beginner to use as it remains tacky indefinitely and is ready to use within 15 minutes of applying. Oil-based size can be ready to use within ten minutes or within several hours, depending on which type is bought. The metal leaf needs to be applied as soon as it becomes tacky and, as it dries quite quickly, timing is crucial.

Duncan Ayscough's exquisitely refined, curvaceously thrown vessels have a rich surface built up with layers of terra sigillata, smoke and waxes. He applies small pools of gold leaf inside the rim, which heighten the visual impact of the interiors and act as a contrast to the mottled reds, greys and black exterior surfaces. He bisque fires to 950°–1050°C (1742°–1922°F) before the smoke firing, which maintains an intense heat over a

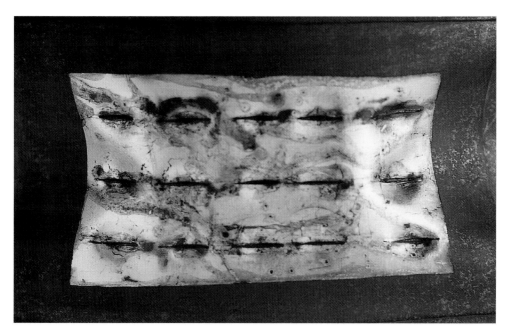

number of days.

Terra sigillata is a slip made of the finest particles of clay, which are separated out and have a natural sheen. It was first used by the Greeks and Romans. A slow sawdust firing over several days enhances the shiny surface with subtle tones of browns through greys to black. The use of gold leaf on the interior contrasts shockingly with the restrained surface of the rest of the form.

Patination with chemicals

Some household substances will cause some patination to metal surfaces and you may wish to experiment with vinegar, salt, lemon juice and toothpaste. However, specialist art suppliers sell chemicals suitable for patination of metal leaf. Potassium sulphide, sodium chloride, copper nitrate, potassium chloride and ammonia are some well-known chemicals used for this purpose. Colours varying from green and turquoise through to

Figure 45 Close-up of a patinated silver surface, piece by Joy Bosworth. (Photo: Dan Bosworth)

Figure 46 Patinating silver leaf with potassium sulphide. (Photo: Dan Bosworth)

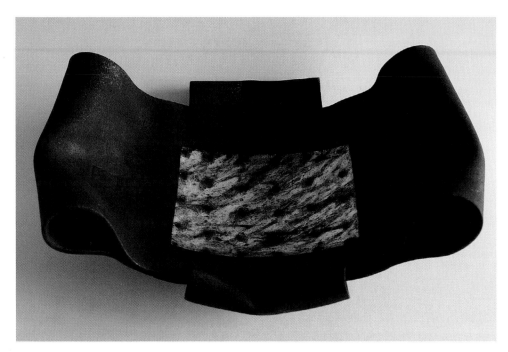

orange, brown, grey and black are possible. The effects and colours vary depending on the type of metal leaf, chemical, its strength, type of application (sponged or brushed) and time of exposure, so it is important to experiment. It is usually better to apply the chemicals in a number of layers to develop an interesting and varied patina. Heat will quicken the patination; some potters use their kiln, others an old gas cooker or a hairdryer. Reactions are 100% faster for every 10 degrees of heat. It is necessary to keep a close watch on the patination process or the surface will turn black or may be damaged by the chemical. When the required result has been achieved, it will be necessary to wash off the chemical, and to dry and then seal the surface from further oxidation with either beeswax or a cellulose or acrylic spray lacquer.

Potassium sulphide gives subtle browns, greys and blacks used at different dilutions and for differing

Figure 47 Finished spot platter by Joy Bosworth. (Photo: Dan Bosworth)

lengths of time. Too strong an application will burn through the metal leaf. Apply with a small paintbrush in different applications while heating with a hairdryer. Continue until the right patina develops. For large quantities or bigger pieces, you may wish to speed up the process by using your kiln or an old gas oven on medium heat for a few minutes, which will give rainbow-coloured haloes around blacker areas, but keep checking every few minutes otherwise the whole area will go black. When the required effect has been achieved, wash off the chemical with running water and leave to dry before masking and spraying with a clear lacquer.

Tony Foard uses patinated silver leaf to enhance his tall, individually modelled, African women (Figure 48), which are fired using various techniques based on conventional raku and smoke firing. He also uses small amounts of glaze and lustre. His work is also shown in Chapter 2 (see Figure 34, on p.35).

The silver leaf is patinated by using two different chemicals, which give different colours: Liberon antiquing fluid (tourmaline) gives muted greys and browns; oxidising concentrate (ammonium hydrosulphide) gives yellows and gold. Foard has developed different ways of working with the chemicals, but a starting point is to wet the surface of the piece and then to apply with a brush a tiny amount of one or both chemicals diluted in warm water, which is left on briefly and then washed off when the right quality is achieved. He puts the wet, patinated work in the kiln at 100°C (212°F), which develops the patination and dries the piece, although care has to be taken not to completely blacken the silver leaf. The patinated silver leaf is then masked and sprayed with a transparent lacquer (either acrylic or cellulose), which is used on the metal and protects it from further oxidisation.

Alasdair MacDonell's work is concerned with a surface texture achieved by patchworking together disparate elements, replicating items collected from beaches, roadsides and 'any other places where the detritus of human activity collects'. He forms the surfaces into masks, some made from a mould taken from his own face, which he alters and elongates. In the piece shown in Figure 49 he has fired to stoneware with glaze and oxides and then coaxed soft pewter foil over the surface of small sections, which are glued, patinated and polished. He often adds other found materials to his finished pieces.

Figure 48 Tony Foard: two African figures, ht: 50cm (20in.).

45

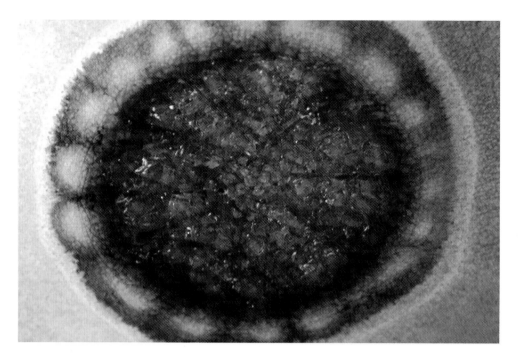

OPPOSITE: **Figure 49** Alasdair MacDonell: *Mask*, 40 × 32cm (16 × 13in.). (Photo: Alasdair MacDonell)

Figure 50 Margaret Smith: detail of glass melted into the surface of a bowl at 1260°C (2300°F). (Photo: Dan Bosworth)

Melted glass surfaces

Window or picture glass softens at around 800°C (1472°F) and melts at 1060°C (1940°F) but may vary from this depending on the size of granules, type of glass and thickness used. Glass will withstand stoneware temperatures but needs to be contained within a well or within deep textures to stop it spilling over onto the kiln shelf. It will crack on cooling, giving a crazed pool that, surprisingly, has a smooth surface and can be used as a decorative device. Coloured bottle glass can be used but may be more prone to faults like bubbling or scumming (when a white, powdery layer of devitrified glass appears).

Oxides and/or glazes can be used with the glass to give colour, and copper or cobalt oxide are very effective too,

giving a beautiful turquoise or blue respectively. It is always best to test glass first before using.

Offcuts of sheet glass can usually be found at picture framers, who are often only too pleased to get rid of their offcuts. If you need to crush the glass into smaller pieces then it needs to be wrapped in ten or so layers of newspaper, placed on the floor and then hammered. Goggles should be worn during this process. Hammered glass fragments can vary from 4mm to dust but if too much glass dust is used, it is more likely to bubble as air will become trapped in the molten glass.

Coloured glass ingots can be bought in some giftware and florist shops; they are normally used to fill and/or decorate glass flower vases but can be a cheap source of coloured glass. Tests need to

Figure 51 Suzie Clark: glass melted onto geological form to suggest image of water. (Photo: Dan Bosworth)

be done, however, as some of them have surface varnishes that will burn away in the kiln. In the piece shown in Figure 50, Margaret Smith has placed ingots in the bottom of an open dish to create a pool of colour when fired to stoneware.

Suzie Clark is interested in the way water runs over geological tracts and has used the qualities of melted glass when fired to 1260°C (2300°F) to run over her sculptural pieces to mimic water. She is careful not to apply too much glass, or it will run down onto the kiln shelf.

Health and safety

Some metals may give off vapours or gases when fired in the kiln so adequate extraction needs to be fitted in the kiln room.

Chemicals are dangerous and may be corrosive. Always read the instructions on the manufacturer's label, and wear goggles and rubber gloves throughout the process. Wash any splashes to the skin immediately with large amounts of water. Always add the chemicals to water – never vice versa. When mixing a chemical with diluted ammonia, add the chemical until no more of it will dissolve. Work in a well-ventilated area. Store chemicals in a locked, dry, cool place, out of the reach of children. Do not eat, drink or smoke in the workshop.

Chapter 4

Electrical

Some ceramic makers have been seduced by the translucency of porcelain or by the play of light through holes in their work, and there is a growing interest in this type of function. While candles can be used to light ceramic work, some contemporary makers wish to use electric light. Margaret O'Rorke is aware that, historically, fire and candles created an atmosphere of warmth and well-being, but in this modern world she feels a need to create lighting schemes that can instantly be activated with clean, easily maintained, up-to-date technology.

Low-voltage halogen lights are small and not intrusive to a design. They give a white light when full on but, when dimmed, spread a warmer, more atmos-pheric light. They come in a wide variety of fittings, light strengths and beam widths. A recent technological innova-tion, electroluminescent panels are safe, non-heat generating and flexible, and can light work in a subtle way. The panels are the thickness of a few sheets of paper, can be used internally and externally, using a choice of power sources, and offer new possibilities for makers.

Margaret O'Rorke was one of the first to explore the possibilities of translu-cency with stunningly lit sculptural pieces and installations, some of which have been site-specific. The thrown elements – made from Audrey Blackman's porcelain, chosen for its translucency –

Health and safety

There are some practical and safety issues to be considered before using electric lighting with ceramics, particularly in the case of pieces that are to be sold. Any electrical components used must satisfy the requirements of the Electrical Equipment (Safety) Regulations 1994.

There are electrical lamp fitment suppliers who will supply craft workers by mail order. They have a statutory duty to supply electrical equipment that satisfies the 1994 regulations and, so long as you do not alter or tamper with these fitments, they will comply. If in doubt, discuss your plans with the local trading standards department or ask an approved and qualified electrician to check over any lamp you have made. For further information read: Department of Trade and Industry, *Electrical Equipment Guidance Notes on UK Regulations July 1995*, reprinted 2000, URN00/588 (available from the DTI, see www.dti.gov.uk).

For bigger installations it would be advisable to work with a lighting consultant. For those living in the UK, contact the National Inspection Council for Electrical Installation to find an approved electrician in your area (see www.niceic.org.uk or telephone 020 7564 2323).

ABOVE: **Figure 52** Margaret O'Rorke: *Big Wheel*, wall light sculpture, translucent porcelain wings, thrown and reformed attached to a metal light box, dia: 100cm (39in.). (Photo: Richard Heeps)

BELOW: **Figure 53** Amy Cooper: three porcelain lamps, ht: 10 × 12cm (4 × 5in.).

which are sometimes cut and distorted, are brought together into a much larger installation. Her firing schedule intensifies the translucency: she heavily reduces at 960°C (1760°F) for one hour, continuing the firing with a light reduction to 1250°C (2282°F) and ending with a period of oxidation up to 1300°C (2372°F). The finely thrown porcelain alters and moves during the firing, something she has learned to accept and that she now uses to her advantage. In the piece shown in Figure 52 she has made individual 'wings', which are joined after firing to an aluminium backing plate in which the electric light is fitted, by means of small holes in the porcelain and stainless steel wire.

Margaret O'Rorke prefers to work with a lighting consultant because of the complications and implications of health and safety legislation with regard to the potential fire risks of poorly installed

Figure 54 Catrin Mostyn Jones. (Photo: Richard Weltman)

electrics. She is currently developing a series of smaller pieces with a domestic environment in mind, which she hopes will be made, to her design, with the collaboration of a manufacturer.

Amy Cooper's porcelain lamps are influenced by microscopic pollen grains and plankton as well as nature on a mighty scale, like volcanoes and icebergs. She casts her forms in porcelain casting slip (supplied by Briar Wheels), and these are then bisque fired to 900°C (1652°F); she 'tidies up' at this stage because the pieces are so delicate when unfired. She then fires the pieces to 1250°C (2282°F) with a soak of ten minutes in an oxidised atmosphere, on a bed of calcined alumina to help prevent slumping and warping. In parts she uses a dry glaze, which crawls due to a magnesium carbonate and nepheline syenite combination, which

51

LEFT: **Figure 55** Elaine Hind: *Leek Flower Head Lamp.* (Photo: Simon Harris)

ABOVE: **Figure 56** Elaine Hind: *Leek Flower Head Lamp*, close-up of lamp when lit.

she sometimes colours with cobalt chloride or oxide, copper carbonate or red iron oxide. Some pieces are enhanced with a satin cream stoneware glaze and some are unglazed and sanded with a diamond pad.

The hole for the electrical fitting is crucial and, when leatherhard, she uses a scalpel to carefully cut a hole exactly 11% bigger than the bung that secures the light fitting, to allow for the shrinkage of the clay. She has found it best to stand the porcelain form in the kiln on the hole to keep it perfectly round and to lessen warping. The bung is a plastic 'money box' lid with a hole drilled through the centre so that the light fitting is held in place inside the porcelain form. She uses a cable grip so that, when changing the bulb, the wiring is not pulled or dislodged. The light fitting is a brass fitting for a 15-watt pygmy bulb (electrical fitments supplied by Collingwood VLM, see the 'Suppliers' section at the back of the book).

Catrin Mostyn Jones's wall light is also inspired by microscopic sea creatures and cell structures, focusing on form and vivid colour. Her work is press-moulded and handbuilt, and bisque fired to

1120°C (2048°F). She uses earthenware glazes, which are applied by spraying multiple layers with areas of wax resist. The light shown (Figure 54) is designed to be wired in to the wall and, made like a bowl, it rests on a lug built into the backing plate to which the light fitting is screwed. A bulb glows through holes within the spikes, creating an atmospheric, sculptural piece rather than a functional light. She works with an electrician who has helped her take into consideration the safety issues of using electricity. (Metal light fitting, brass lamp holds and male cord grips are supplied by Specialist Lamp Fitting Suppliers; see the 'Suppliers' section at the back of the book.)

Elaine Hind's tall standing lamp (Figure 55) is based on the flower heads of leek plants that have gone to seed. Made from a porcelain/T-material mix, which is not translucent, it is coloured with underglaze colours and copper carbonate under a satin dolomite glaze and fired to 1260°C (2300°F). The dome of the seed head lifts off, revealing the electrical light fitting for ease of bulb-changing, and the wire runs down the hollow ceramic stem passing through a hole at the bottom of the stand at the end of which is attached the plug.

When the light is switched on (Figure 56), tiny holes glow with escaping light, some of which are embellished with coloured glass 'seeds', casting beautiful patterns on surrounding walls and ceiling.

Beth Marriott is interested in the way previously ordinary objects are transformed after someone close dies. The stuff of the person's everyday life, like a shampoo bottle or toothbrush, becomes precious and a room can become a shrine. In this conceptual, sculptural piece (*Transformation I*) she has created slipcast porcelain replicas of everyday plastic bottles and put them in a domestic setting; she has given them a 'halo' of light from beneath to suggest their enhanced meaning. Holes were made in the table into which electric light fitments and bulbs were secured; the ceramic bottles rest over them, allowing light to glow around their bases.

Figure 57 Beth Marriott: *Transformation I.*

53

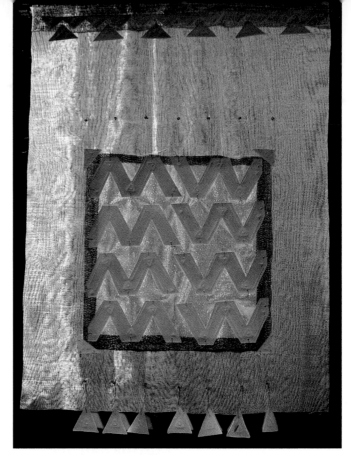

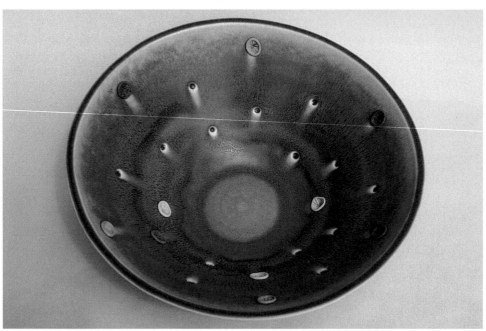

Chapter 5

Textiles

Combining simple textile techniques with ceramics offers opportunities to explore their opposing tactile properties, and the softness and texture of textiles can be mimicked by clay. Expensive equipment does not initially need to be bought as simple weaving can be done on a sheet of firm, smooth cardboard or over a box; dyeing can be done in a saucepan on the stove or in a washing machine; and felting can be done on a tabletop or in the hand.

Lugs or holes

Makers like Polly and Garry Utley have been inspired by the colour and texture of Indian textiles; they make ceramic wall pieces and vessels that combine tassels, ribbon and braid with the clay once it is fired, by the use of lugs or holes. Lugs or holes need to be made in the ceramic piece in readiness for the textile part to be joined, but because of the flexibility of the textile element and its inclusion after the ceramic piece has been fired, detailed measuring does not need to be done in advance, except to make sure that the lug or hole is placed correctly and is strong and big enough, taking into account the shrinkage that occurs during drying and firing.

OPPOSITE (TOP): **Figure 58** Elizabeth Smith: *Afra*.

OPPOSITE (BOTTOM): **Figure 59** Monica Sinclair-Smith: bowl with coloured rubber, w: 31cm (12in.), ht: 9cm (3.5in.).

Elizabeth Smith makes holes in her translucent bone china pieces, fired to 1240°C (2264°F), and joins them together with 34-gauge brass beading wire. She has used dark green organza and fine single gold fabric to complete the delicate wall hanging in Figure 58, the translucency of which is highlighted when shown hanging against a window.

Monica Sinclair-Smith has made holes in this slipcast bowl (Figure 59), fired to 1260°C (2300°F) with a barium glaze, to take the colourful rubber balloon tails that are pushed through the holes after firing and held in place by being wrapped around metal washers.

Textile handles

Embroidery silk comes in a wide range of colours that can be used to complement the colours in the ceramic piece or as a contrast. The sequence of pictures on pp.56–58 (Figures 60–65) illustrates two ways of using embroidery thread to make handles.

Owen Wall has developed both an aesthetic and functional handle (Figure 66) using traditional methods with modern materials. The black nylon webbing used for the handle covers plastic tubing, cut as if it was for a bamboo handle, then the end is passed through the lug on the teapot and held together with plastic cable ties. He has found that the plastic tubing softens with the heat from the tea and has modified the design to incorporate an inner handle made of steel soldered into place around the lugs.

55

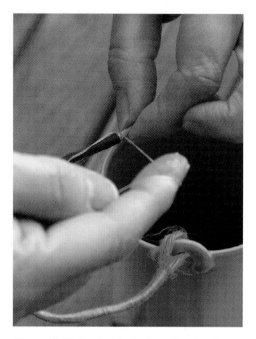

Making a bound handle
Figure 60 Start by making a loop.

Figure 61 Bind towards the loop, keeping the work tight.

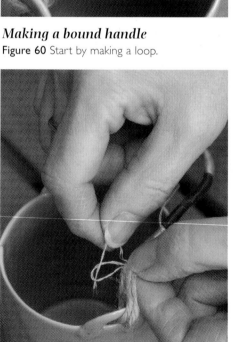

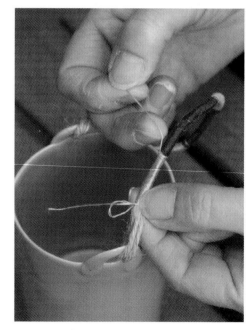

Figure 62 Poke the end through the loop.

Figure 63 Pull the loop through to the middle of the bound section so that the ends are held in place and can be cut off.

Figure 64 A group of porcelain vessels with bound and woven handles. (All photos on pp.56–58: Dan Bosworth)

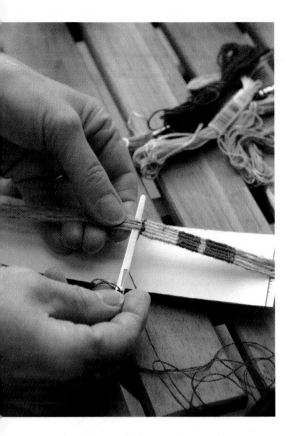

Making a woven handle

Cut 'V' shapes 1cm (0.4in.) deep at the top and bottom of a piece of firm, smooth card, 14–15cm (5.5–6in.) longer than the required handle. Wind string around the card lengthways to fit in to the cut 'V' shapes, which makes the warp, and secure to the back of the card with sticky tape. Tie the end of two strands of embroidery thread about 90cm (35in.) long to no. 2 warp. Using a blunt darning needle, weave in and out of the warp one way, and out and in of the warp on the next row, creating a woven texture. Allow the end to be woven in with the main weaving. If narrow bands of colour are required, do not tie off the end of the colour band but lay it along no. 2 warp and weave it in until it is required for weaving another band of colour. When the weaving is long enough for the handle, cut off and tie through the lugs of the pot.

Figure 65 Woven handle made on a simple cardboard loom.

The webbing tags protruding through slits on each side of the thrown plates shown in Figure 67 are held in place by melting the end into a lump, which is hidden under the turned back foot.

Felting

Merino fleece felts the best and can be bought in natural colours or already dyed in a variety of colours in 100g (0.2lb) bags from wool suppliers by mail order; 250g (0.5lb) bags of mixed colours can be bought in a selection of complementary colours (i.e. pinks, purples and blues). Small amounts of natural fleece can be found hanging on fences surrounding fields in which sheep graze. Woollen fleece that has been felted properly will not fray when cut and can be made in varying thicknesses.

To make a piece of felt you will need:
- fleece
- rush beach mat
- square of fabric slightly smaller than the beach mat's width
- diluted washing-up liquid.

Working on a worktop or table that will not be damaged by water, lay the beach mat down and then the fabric over the top. The rough texture of the beach mat creates friction and speeds up the felting process. Teased-out lengths of fleece are placed in one direction, over the fabric, leaving a border of about 4cm (1½in.). Repeat the process, but lay the fleece on top of the previous layer in the other direction. You will need three to five layers for an average thickness.

Figure 66 Owen Wall: teapot with nylon webbing handle. (Photo: Bob Heffil)

Figure 67 Owen Wall: thrown/turned plates with webbing tag handles. (Photo: Bob Heffil)

Different-coloured fleece can be used and other natural fibres can be felted by adding a very thin layer of woollen fleece over to attach them. Drizzle the diluted washing-up liquid over the fleece. Roll the 'sandwich' up in the beach mat, rolling backwards and forwards against the work surface for five minutes. Unroll and add more washing-up liquid if it seems a bit dry, but do not wet too much or water will be running everywhere. Turn the fabric and fleece round on the beach mat and roll up again. Roll backwards and forwards for a further five minutes. Repeat the process at least one more time, which will make the felting time at least 15 minutes, by when the fleece should adhere together into a felt-type fabric. More time will be needed if the fibres have not felted. You can make a more robust fabric by sewing it within a muslin pocket and putting it in a washing machine on a hot-wash cycle; this will cause the felt to become harder and to shrink considerably.

Felt knob for a raku sphere

The sequence of pictures (Figures 68–71) illustrates a method for making a felt knob for a raku sphere.

Take a small bundle of wool and moisten it with diluted washing-up liquid. Roll it back and forth in the palms of the hands for five minutes. The fibres will become matted and stick together into a small sphere. Experience will show how much wool is needed for the size of bobble required. When dry, the bobble can be used in jewellery pieces as a deco-rative element or as a knob on a ceramic piece as seen here.

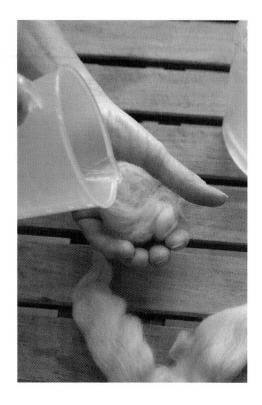

ABOVE: **Figure 68** Wet a small lump of fleece with diluted washing-up liquid.

OPPOSITE, TOP LEFT: **Figure 69** Roll the fleece between the palms of the hands for a few minutes.

OPPOSITE, TOP RIGHT: **Figure 70** It will become a hardened felt ball.

Figure 71 (RIGHT:) The felt knob can be attached with ribbon through a hole in the lid.

(All photos on pp.60–61: Dan Bosworth)

Figure 72 Kathy Williams and Jan Beeny: *Ewe*.

Kathy Williams makes kumihimo braids from lumpy, handmade yarns using natural fleece, and these are used to represent the woolly coat of this ewe (Figure 72). Jan Beeny makes the heads and beads for these collaborative pieces, which she colours with oxides and stoneware glaze.

Ceramic buttons

Ceramic buttons are an obvious way of bringing together the two materials and can effectively embellish either hand-made or manufactured garments, cushions or bags.

Making a plaster mould for buttons

Figures 73–76 illustrate a method for making a shell-shaped plaster mould for buttons.

Figure 73 Bury a shell halfway into some clay, creating no undercuts. (All photos pp.63–64: Dan Bosworth)

Figure 74 Build a wall around the clay and shell, and pour plaster on top.

Figure 75 The finished plaster mould with clay shell impression.

A small mould can be made from a shell, which is set into clay exposing the part that will become the button.

Wrap a length of plastic or stiff paper (this is known as a cottle) around the shell/clay and hold in place with tape, sealing it with clay around the base and inside, around the edge between the cottle and the clay. Estimate how much volume of plaster you will need to cover the shell and give a thickness to the mould of about 10cm (4in.). Pour about half that quantity of water into a bowl. Sprinkle the plaster over the surface of the water until islands are built up on the surface that do not sink. Wait a few moments to let the plaster absorb water, then gently agitate the plaster/water mix without introducing air and making sure there are no lumps. When the plaster begins to thicken, pour it gently over the prepared shell. When the plaster has gone hard, within 15 minutes or so, the cottle can be removed.

The clay and shell are removed to reveal the mould, which is used for press-moulding when it is fully dry. A 'sausage' of clay is formed into a lug and attached with slip to the back of the shell, making it into a button.

Tessa Wolfe-Murray uses sweet cutters to cut her smoke-fired buttons. They are coloured with slips before bisque firing to 1120°C (2048°F) and then smoked by burning wood shavings soaked in white spirit in selected areas.

Kay Cartwright's buttons are also made with sweet cutters, and are coloured with underglazes and transparent glaze and fired to 1120°C (2048°F).

Susan Nemeth's buttons, made from offcuts, are made of coloured porcelain agateware, fired to cone 9.

Figure 76 Buttons by Tessa Wolfe-Murray, Susan Nemeth, Kay Cartwright and Joy Bosworth.

The shell buttons shown in Figure 76 were fired to earthenware with a transparent glaze and then fired to 750°C (1382°F) with a mother-of-pearl lustre.

Fabric dyes

Chemical dyes can be bought at a large number of high-street outlets. Silk dyes and textile paints can be bought in art shops but a more detailed investigation is necessary if vegetable dyes are to be used.

Natural fibres like cotton, wool and linen take colour best, but some synthetic materials will take dye. Dyes can be bought for use in a washing machine, microwave or rustproof saucepan with cold, hand-hot or simmering water. It is important to look at the manufacturer's instructions for types of dye, fabric, method and duration of dyeing. The original colour of the fabric to be dyed will affect the final colour achieved (for example, blue dye on yellow fabric will give green). The fabric can be tied up in bundles with string or with elastic bands, which will resist the dye and prevent it from affecting the areas around which they are tied – this is known as tie-dying. Dyes can also be used to colour wood, grasses and feathers.

The jewellery in Figure 77 combines dyed muslin, raku-fired tubes and beads, and handmade silver findings.

The pouches in Figure 78 were made to cover, reflect and enhance delicate, sculptural 'soul-sticks' made in smoked clay. Muslin was dyed with pastel-coloured cold dyes. When dry, it was cut into pieces, reassembled and top-stitched with thread of a contrasting colour. A buttonhole entrance allowed the soul-stick to enter the pouch and it could not be seen once inside. A ceramic handle for each pouch was raku fired and the pouch stitched to it.

65

ABOVE: **Figure 77** Joy Bosworth: dyed muslin, silver and ceramic jewellery. (Photo: Dan Bosworth)

BELOW: **Figure 78** Joy Bosworth: pouches for soul-sticks (detail). (Photo: Dan Bosworth)

Figure 79 Virginia Graham: *Feather Teapot.*

ABOVE: **Figure 80** Sue Clews: woven plastic-covered wire basket with raku beads for raku cup with yellow glaze. (Photo: Dan Bosworth)

BELOW: **Figure 81** Tineke van Gils: handsewn red silk bag with black cord pull to protect white thrown porcelain tea caddies.

Virginia Graham makes humorous, postmodern pieces (like that in Figure 79) that make reference to the qualities found in slipcast, industrial tableware. She uses white stoneware slipcast and handbuilt elements joined with black slip, and applies commercial transfer prints and lustres over a transparent glaze. She juxtaposes with panache the industrial and the handbuilt qualities, adding the finishing touch of a dyed black feather.

Bags

Sue Clews uses a self-invented method that is part weaving, part sewing, part knitting, to make this 'basket' (Figure 80) using recycled telephone wire. She starts at the base of the 'basket' and forms a loop, then works around the base, increasing loops to make the required shape for the base. When the base is the correct size, the wire is bent upwards to form the walls of the 'basket', stretching and forming to keep the shape even and the loops regular. The raku beads are placed randomly during the making process. In Figure 80 this method is seen over a raku-fired pot with a yellow glaze to match the yellow wire of the basket.

Tineke van Gils, the Dutch maker, also likes the idea of using a bag to protect something that is small and fragile. She makes beautiful hand-sewn red-silk bags to protect her white, thrown porcelain tea caddies, reinforcing the feeling of preciousness.

The shoulder bag in Figure 82, made as 'wearable art', brings together porcelain, glass and textured knitting yarn. The spiky texture is achieved by pushing a plaster die stamp into a moist disc of porcelain, which is then applied to the backing panel and fired to 1260°C (2300°F). The colour is achieved by melting glass onto the surface. A fluffy knitted lining and handle bring the piece together.

Figure 82 Ulrike Mueller: *Orange.*

Chapter 6

Glass

Claire Ireland has successfully combined a manufactured glass bowl in this humorous assemblage called *Fish Charmer* (Figure 83), but ceramic makers can use some of the skills and equipment they already have to make kiln-formed glass. Potters also have some of the qualities necessary for working with glass: patience, tenacity and commitment to an elongated process that ultimately relies on the kiln for results.

It can be interesting to experiment with glass with little extra expense. Scrap glass can sometimes be obtained free from picture framers, as noted earlier, coloured bottle glass can be collected, coloured glass ingots/beads can be bought cheaply from florist or gift shops, and shattered safety glass can be gathered from vandal-ised bus shelters (being very careful and wearing gloves, of course). If scrap glass is being used, it needs to be tested in the kiln for compatibility and colour. For those who are more serious about its use in their work, glass suppliers sell glass of different types, in sheets of different thick-nesses, rod and grain, all in many colours that are compatible with each other. Different types and thicknesses of glass behave in different ways in the kiln, but here are a few important and funda-mental considerations to bear in mind prior to experimentation.

OPPOSITE: **Figure 83** Claire Ireland: *Fish Charmer*, assemblage – glass bowl, fish, pebbles, weed and ceramic stoneware figure. (Photo: Kit Young)

General rules

One can never be absolutely sure what is going to happen in the kiln, but with experience, glass can be coaxed to behave in a predictable way. Here are some useful pointers.

- An electric kiln with an electronic programmer is best for firing glass. The kiln should be clean and free from dust during firing. Glass should also be clean, as dust and fingerprints will contribute to devitrification (a crystalline build-up that looks like a white hue) forming on the surface during firing.
- Glass sheet should be of the same thickness when fusing, otherwise stresses will cause cracks either in the kiln or at a later stage.
- Different pieces of glass that are to be fused together should be compatible – that is, they should have the same fusing/melting temperature and coefficients of expansion.
- Larger and thicker pieces of glass are more likely to crack and will need careful annealing.

Annealing glass

Annealing is advisable when firing glass, in order to balance the stresses caused by the uneven extreme/internal tempera-ture within the glass that occurs during firing, as this lessens the likelihood of cracking. Annealing is the careful control of temperature at the point when melting begins to occur during heating and when the glass begins to solidify during cooling. This temperature varies with different thicknesses and types of glass. The glass supplier will know the annealing temperature of the glass sold, but here are a couple of examples.

- Soda lime glass: annealing temperature 525°–552°C (977–1026°F).
- Full lead crystal: annealing temperature 420°–450°C (788–842°F).

Slumping glass

Glass that is unsupported will begin to bend between 560°C –650°C (1040°–1202°F), and if it is balanced over or in a mould will slump into the form of the mould. Simple, shallow moulds are more easy to use to begin with, as gravity may cause the glass to fold over or sag if steeper-sided moulds are used. The thicker and larger the piece of glass, the harder it is to control effects in the kiln and careful annealing is paramount. Thicknesses up to 6mm (0.24in.) can be fired without too many problems. Thinner glass can sometimes be fired in smaller pieces without annealing, by closing the bungs at 520°C (968°) for soda lime glass and at 420°C (788°F) for lead crystal and allowing the kiln to cool naturally.

Potters usually use plaster of Paris for moulds when slipcasting and hand-building, but for use inside the kiln other ingredients need to be added to give strength and durability. Such a mould can be used in the kiln on many occasions so long as it is not moved from the kiln shelf on which it is supported. For repeat use, a mould made out of bisque-fired clay is advised, coated with alumina batt wash to act as a separator, or with alumina paper covering the surface.

Additions to plaster for mould-making to be used inside the kiln

- Flint is used by potters in glazes and gives strength to moulds for use inside the kiln when added to plaster.
- Investrite is a crystobolite used by jewellers for casting and is used in moulds for higher temperatures.
- HT aggregate is a high-alumina refractory substance that will contaminate the surface of glass if allowed to come in contact with it in the kiln. When used in a recipe in which it comprises no more than one-third of materials, it is adequately coated by the other ingredients and does not cause problems of contamination.

Keith Cummings, in his book *Techniques of Kiln Formed Glass* (1997), gives the following simple recipes for making moulds.

600°–700°C (1112°–1292°F)
At this temperature glass can be bent into simple moulds.

Plaster	50 parts
Flint or quartz	50 parts

700°–800°C (1292°–1472°F)
At this temperature glass can be fused and will take on complex textures from moulds. Pâte-de-verre can be made at this temperature.

Plaster	33.3 parts
Investrite	33.3 parts
HT aggregate	33.3 parts (80s mesh)

800°–975°C (1472°–1787°F)
At temperatures between 800°C and 975°C, when the glass is most liquid, the mould needs to be made from this recipe with the further protection of an outer

receptacle. This is done by placing the mould into a ceramic saggar or metal container, and packing the space between the two with silver sand.

Making a mould for a simple bowl

Figures 84–86 illustrate a method for making a mould for a simple bowl.

RIGHT: **Figure 84** A thrown hump of clay.

BELOW LEFT: **Figure 85** Make a cottle around the clay hump, which is sealed inside and out with clay. Mix plaster/flint and pour into prepared cottle, when beginning to go off.

BELOW RIGHT: **Figure 86** Take off the cottle and pull out the clay to reveal the plaster mould. (All photos: Dan Bosworth)

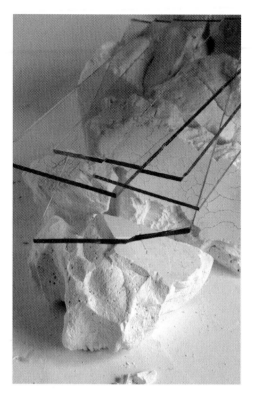

Figure 87 Suzie Clarke: plaster fragments resting on a kiln shelf prepared with alumina batt wash, and slithers of scrap glass balanced on top. (Photo: Dan Bosworth)

Figure 88 Suzie Clarke: slumped glass mimicking water splashing over rocks. (Photo: Dan Bosworth)

Mixing the ingredients for mould-making

The dry ingredients should be mixed when dry, and this should be done inside a spray booth, wearing a mask because of the hazardous nature of the substances. When mould-making for glass you should make the mixture more dense than when making moulds for ceramics. The dry ingredients are sprinkled over the surface of the water and 20% less water will be necessary than when using plaster alone. Ruth Lyne uses 700ml (1.2 pints) of water to 900g (1.9lb) dry ingredients.

Suzie Clarke (Figure 87 and 88) uses 2mm (⅟₁₆in.) soda lime float (picture) glass, slumped over kiln-fired plaster fragments at 800°C (1472°F) to suggest the way water tumbles and cascades over rocks. Plaster of Paris, when fired in the kiln, cracks with interesting 'geological' surfaces, which in this case, have been used creatively.

Making a slumped glass lid for a vessel

Figures 89–93 illustrate a method used by Ruth Lyne and Joy Bosworth when making a slumped glass lid for a vessel.

LEFT: **Figure 89** Roll out a piece of clay 2.5cm (1in.) thick and press it over the top of the bisque-fired pot. Press into opening on pot.

BELOW LEFT: **Figure 90** Turn over onto a doughnut of clay, which will support the form. Integrate the wall of the mould, making sure it is strong enough to hold the liquid plaster.

BELOW RIGHT: **Figure 91** Gently take out the pot, making sure you do not distort the mould. Fill with plaster/flint mix using 450g (0.9lb) plaster and 450g (0.9lb) flint, mixed with 700ml (1.2 pints) water. (See moulds recipes for use inside kiln and mixing methods on pp.72–73.)

(All photos on pp.75–76: Dan Bosworth)

Fusing glass

Glass becomes liquid between 760°C (1400°F) and 800°C (1472°F), and pieces of glass will stick together at this point. Finer grades of crushed glass will require a higher temperature on the basis of surface-to-mass ratio. Alumina mixed with water to a painting consistency and painted on kiln shelves stops glass sticking to them. This leaves an

LEFT: **Figure 92** Turn over and release the plaster hump from the clay. The fused glass is balanced on top of the hump mould in the kiln and fired to 730°C (1346°F) so that it will take on the form of the plaster.

BELOW: **Figure 93** Finished raku-fired pot with slumped glass lid that locates over the pot opening.

uneven surface on the glass when fired, which you may think adds character to a piece. If a smooth surface is required, however, it is possible to make a smooth batt from plaster of Paris and flint in equal proportions, and cast onto a glass or smooth metal surface. A smear of oil will act as a separator, stopping the cast plaster batt from sticking to the smooth surface.

Different materials can be trapped between layers of glass to decorative effect. Try experiments with precious metal leaf, aluminium foil, fine copper wire, metal gauze, washers, paper, fabric or leaves. The larger and thicker the inclusion, the more likely it is that cracks and air bubbles will occur. Inclusions may remain fairly unaltered when trapped between the glass layers, may become altered by oxidisation or may leave an ash 'ghost' of the object.

Elaine Hind

In the sculptural ceramic and glass electric lamp shown in Figure 94, Elaine Hind uses 2mm (0.08in.) coloured glass slivers fused together in the kiln to suggest the seeds on the beautiful flower heads of leeks. When the lamp is lit, these create dramatic shadows on surrounding walls. Because the slivers of glass to be fused are so small, Hind does not need to anneal during firing, and fires to 750°–760°C (1382–1400°F), depending on the colour desired. She uses a tiny dab of PVA glue to secure the slivers in the kiln, which burns away during firing. If too much PVA is used to stick glass together in the kiln a dark residue is left. The glass 'seeds' are secured to the ceramic globe once all the elements are fired, using PVA glue, which is transparent when dry and has proved to be strong enough, even after

Figure 94 Elaine Hind: *Leek Flower Head Lamp*, (detail). (Photo: Simon Harris)

five years. She chooses not to use epoxy resin because it is messy and becomes more yellow as time passes.

Ruth Lyne (see Figure 95) uses horticultural glass for her pieces because it is hand rolled. She finds that window glass, which has been 'floated' onto sheets of tin, leaves a residue on the glass. This residue reacts unpleasantly with silver, copper and gold leaf, which she traps between two sheets of glass, altering the colours achieved. When the horticultural glass is fired to 830°C (1526°F) the two sheets completely fuse together, making an even, rounded edge, and the pattern created with the precious metal

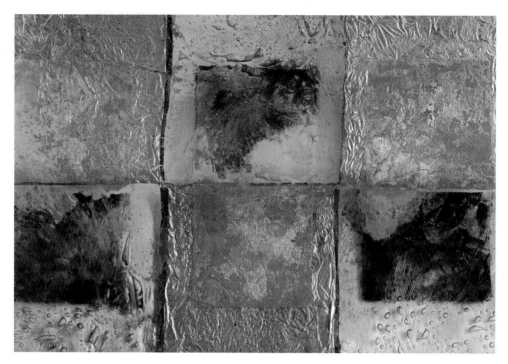

Figure 95 Ruth Lyne: precious metal leaf trapped between two layers of glass. (Photo: Dan Bosworth)

fully preserved. She soaks the kiln at 560°C (1040°F) for half an hour to anneal the glass, which is made of two 3mm (⅛in.) sheets, giving an overall thickness of 6mm (¼in.).

In Figure 96, soda lime float glass is crushed with a hammer between sheets of newspaper and sieved into a mould prepared with a copper collar, which is joined with handmade rivets. (Always wear goggles when crushing glass.) When the glass is fused together at 840°C (1544°F), it becomes attached to the copper collar. This piece was not annealed when the kiln reached temperature, and was allowed to cool naturally with the bungs in. The surface of the copper collar becomes oxidised in the kiln. This could be cleaned off with diluted sulphuric acid ('pickle'). A

separate copper rim and collar was made and coloured with borax flux, which turns copper red when melted. Gold glass lustre was painted in a line around the glass rim and re-fired to 650°C (1202°F). The whole piece was assembled with the ceramic cone (Figure 97) using a chemical bonding material.

Pâte-de-verre

This process – whose name means, literally, 'paste of glass' – uses granular glass, held together with glue or paste, to line a mould to a thickness of 1cm (⅜in.), which is then fused together in the kiln. Diluted gum arabic or wallpaper paste will hold the grains of glass together until fused and will burn away in the kiln. Grains of different sizes and colours, which are designed to be compatible, can be bought from suppliers. Lead glass is softer and the granules are more likely to fuse together easily, while soda lime (picture) glass is harder and the surface of the fired work will remain more granular in character. Scrap glass crushed between layers of newspaper with a hammer can be used for pâte-de-verre, but this needs to be tested for good results. Crushed safety glass can be made to fuse together and its much larger grains will have a distinctive appearance. While it is easier to use shallow moulds for pâte-de-verre, you may wish to experiment by filling deeper moulds with ceramic fibre or pulverised

RIGHT: **Figure 96** Crushed glass heaped in mould showing copper collar held in place with handmade rivets. (Photo: Dan Bosworth)

BELOW: **Figure 97** Vinod Govindbhai and Joy Bosworth: finished ceramic cone with glass rim. (Photo: Dan Bosworth)

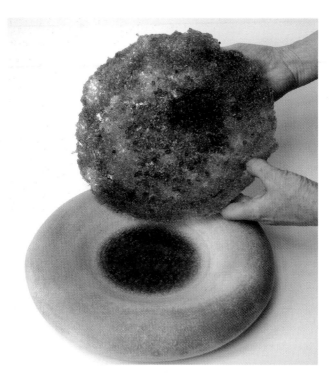

LEFT: **Figure 98** Ruth Lyne and Joy Bosworth: pâte-de-verre bowl with ceramic and melted glass stand. (Photo: Dan Bosworth)

BELOW: **Figure 99** Leonora Minto: pâte-de-verre tops for ceramic slipcast bases.

mould material to hold the glass in place in steeper-sided moulds.

Ruth Lyne has used different-sized granules of glass in compatible glass of the same colour to make the pâte-de-verre bowl in Figure 98. The same glass was used to melt into the surface of the ceramic stand, fired to 1260°C (2300°F).

Leonora Minto carves back-to-front letters and words into a plaster blocks, and sprinkles oxides and powdered glass over the plaster surface. She fuses this together at 820°C (1508°F), leaving an irregular edge and an aged surface. She bonds the glass and ceramic together with a chemical bonding substance easily bought in DIY shops.

Grinding glass

Glass will sometimes need grinding to alter or smooth a piece or to make a hole, and electric tools are available for this purpose. Always use goggles

Figure 100 Jill J. Burns: lidded jars with kiln-formed glass lids, and copper and ceramic handles.

and a mask when grinding.

Jill Burns uses float (window) glass, which she slumps into a mould made of bisque-fired clay, coated with a very thin layer of alumina batt wash. She prefers to use a bisque-fired ceramic mould because the slumped glass picks up the texture of the clay, which integrates it with the rest of the piece. She grinds the lids to fit the fired ceramic jars with first a rough then a smooth grinding bit. A hole is ground into the centre to house the thrown ceramic knob, which is attached with a nut and bolt.

Glass lid firing schedule
- Climb 167°C (333°F)/hour until 537°C (999°F).
- Climb 537°C (999°F)/hour until 793°C (1459°F), hold for 15 minutes.

- Drop 537°C (999°F)/hour until 551°C (1024°F), hold 1 hour.
- Drop 10°C (18°F)/hour, until 482°C (900°F).
- Cool to room temperature.

Combining glass and ceramics in the kiln

Glass can be melted onto the surface of ceramics at stoneware temperatures (as described in Chapter 6), but some makers are exploring ways of combining pieces of glass with clay during the making process. Felicity Aylieff brings together fragments of coloured clay, balontini and borosilicate glass as aggregates into her clay body when making her large-scale ceramic sculptures. She fires to 1000°C (1832°F), and needs to grind and polish the surfaces after firing.

Gwen Bainbridge has also done some research into the use of granules of glass (a little larger than sugar granules) mixed into bone china casting slip. The cast vessels are fired to 1230°C (2246°F) in an electric kiln with a 90-minute soak. The glass particles melt, creating bubbles on the surface that are delicate and potentially hazardous. The surface needs to be ground and polished to make it safe.

Health and safety
Glass has sharp edges that can easily cause cuts and injuries; small chips are not easily seen and can cause damage to the eyes. Goggles should be worn when cutting or crushing glass. Some of the processes described in this chapter, such as mould-making, create dusts that are hazardous. Always comply with the manufacturer's recommendations. When grinding glass or ceramics, it should be done in a spray booth, and goggles and a mask should be worn. Overalls, goggles and masks should be worn whenever this is recommended by the manufacturer. Food and drink should not be consumed in the workshop.

OPPOSITE: **Figure 101** Gwen Bainbridge: glass and ceramic slipcast vessels.

84

Chapter 7

Wood

Most people know what a saw or a chisel is, and will probably know what a lathe is. Most people will also know for what purpose these tools are used. Those who make slipcast ceramics may have used similar tools for shaping a plaster model when mould-making. This chapter presents some simple woodworking techniques, as well as some examples of how contemporary makers are including wood with their ceramic work.

You may be able to find a corner in your ceramics studio for woodwork, but tools need a warm, dry space as they will rust in a damp atmosphere and glue will take longer to dry. Hand tools can be bought as and when you need them and, although power tools speed up jobs, it is possible to do beautiful work without them. Maintenance of woodworking tools is essential and sharp tools are imperative for accurate work.

Some makers have the ideas but not the skills, time or tools necessary to bring them to life, and so collaborate with others. Kate Schuricht has learned the woodworking techniques of cutting, planing, joining and finishing, but she required this box (Figure 103) to be made to such exacting standards that

OPPOSITE: **Figure 102** Bridget Drakeford: porcelain teapot with copper glaze, and rosewood and silver handle. (Photo: Colin Barratt)

RIGHT: **Figure 103** Kate Schuricht/David Gregson: raku vessels in sycamore box 49 × 22 × 11cm (19 × 9 × 4.5in.).

she was unable to give the time to making it. For this reason, she decided to collaborate with furniture maker David Gregson. She is interested in the idea of containment, the rituals of collecting and the placing of special objects. Her slipcast, minimalist, lidded cylinders are raku fired, giving variation to the surface with a distinctive, random crackle in the glaze. She binds them closed to 'protect the inner space and contents'.

The collection of vessels in Figure 103 is protected by an immaculately crafted sycamore box, which has an opening in the lid revealing their existence.

Carving and forming wood

Some makers use wood to make functional handles that enhance and bestow individuality on the style of their work.

The handle shown in Figure 104 was drawn out onto a piece of ash, which is a hard, close-grained wood. It has been drawn diagonally across the grain to give

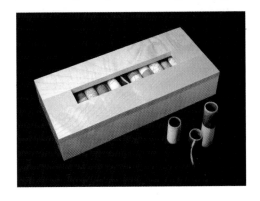

ABOVE: **Figure 104** Forming a wooden handle for a teapot. (Photo: Dan Bosworth)

BELOW: **Figure 105** Steve Harrison: wooden-handled teapots.

strength to the part of the handle that takes the most stress. Forming and shaping a piece of wood for a handle or knob can be done with a combination of tools, including bandsaw, coping saw, carving chisels, rasps, knives and smoothing devices.

The attention to detail and craftsmanship shown in Steve Harrison's wooden handles (Figure 105) reflect the precision of the thrown, salt-glazed teapots to which they fit. He uses ebony and other

Figure 106 Chris Keenan: reduction-fired porcelain teapot with bound cane handle, height 20cm (8in.). (Photo: Stephen Brayne)

hard woods of 'instrument quality', cuts with a coping saw and carves with chisels and knives in the same way one would shape a plaster model for mould-making. The handles are fitted into silver collars with a lug and rivet device, as described in detail in Chapter 2.

The rosewood and silver handle shown in Figure 102 (the picture used to open this chapter) has been developed by Bridget Drakeford to enhance her thrown porcelain teapot, fired to stoneware with a copper glaze. The wooden uprights of the handle are drilled and a threaded silver rod runs through it and into a hole in the teapot, being attached with a silver nut inside the pot. It is possible to remove the handle for washing. In making the handles of her teapots, she collaborates with craftsman friends who have specific skills.

The simplicity of Chris Keenan's tenmoku-glazed, reduction-fired, thrown Limoges porcelain teapots is given distinction by their dyed cane handles. He uses cold fabric dyes in water, which softens the cane, before vigorously winding it into individual handles.

The Russian ceramicist, Igor Khartchenko studied painting and ceramic sculpture, and has travelled widely, being particularly influenced by Mayan and archaic Japanese sculpture. He makes large sculptural 'artefacts', which he slab-builds in white clay, decorated with slips, and fires to 1100°– 1150°C (2012–2102°F). His structures have strong, painted and dyed wood or bamboo handles that he binds onto the ceramic piece with leather, string or rope, which he also marks and dyes.

Wood turning

In turning, a lathe holds and rotates the wood while the maker forms the shape using chisels that are supported on a tool rest positioned in front. When buying a lathe, it is necessary to make sure that the 'bed', or space, that accommodates the workpiece is long enough for your needs. It is also important to buy the most solid and stable lathe you can

afford and that the 'swing' (maximum diameter of the workpiece) is at least 40cm (16in.).

Using a lathe to create a wooden base

Figures 108–11 illustrate the use of a lathe in the creation of a wooden base for a terracotta pot.

Chris Nangle makes solid wood furniture and more sculptural forms for use as tables, seats or benches for interiors or for use in gardens; he also makes smaller 'chilli' bowls. He collaborated in the piece shown in Figures 108–111, making a stand for a spherical terracotta vessel.

He attached a block of oak, off-centre, onto the facing plate of the lathe and then, resting the sharp chisel against the tool rest, turned a bowl shape and surrounding ridges. Chris was working with an oblong block and had to be careful with the chisel as it came to the edges or it could have been thrown out of his hand. The form was then burned with a torch to soften the edges and to bring out the grain. It was brushed vigorously with a wire brush and waxed with dark oak or mahogany beeswax before buffing with a cloth. The terracotta vessel was burnished, once fired to 1060°C (1940°F) then soaked in an inch of strong cold tea for approximately four hours, during which time the tannin rose up the vessel walls as the liquid soaked into it, emphasising the burnishing marks. When dry it was polished with beeswax, which gives a look of leather to the surface.

Sally MacDonell has seated her three smoke-fired figures (Figure 113) on a charred block of wood.

OPPOSITE: **Figure 107** Igor Khartchenko: *Artefact.*

Figure 108 Wood attached to facing plate in off-centre position being formed with chisel.

Figure 109 Formed bowl attached to lathe, facing plate.

Figure 110 Burning surface to blacken.

Figure 111 Finished terracotta pot with wooden base. (All photos: Dan Bosworth)

Recycled wood or driftwood

A number of makers are including recycled or driftwood in their work because the qualities of the two materials complement each other; some make reference to history, journeys or memory.

Sarah Walton is known for salt-glazed ceramics but this bird bath (Figure 112) is made from red earthenware vitrified at 1200°C (2192°F). It is square and boulder-like, prompted by her love for the landscape of the South Downs and the Lake District. The piece looks solid and monumental but is actually hollow and made in a two-piece mould with a small hole in the base. She likes the fact that there is no glaze and that the high-fired red clay reflects light in an entirely different way from the salt-glazed pieces.

Figure 112 Sarah Walton: bird bath.

Figure 113 Sally MacDonell: *Three Figures*, on charred wooden block; ht: 40cm (16in.).

The bird bath stands on a recycled timber pedestal made from eroded pine, Douglas fir or teak, the simplicity of which quietly elevates the work.

When making her bird baths, Walton starts from the piece of wood and alters each bath by modelling so that the two elements work together. A wooden plug 5.1cm (2in.) tall, protrudes above the base and locates through the hole in the bottom of the bird bath, holding it in position.

Elizabeth Elston uses driftwood to frame her flat ceramic pieces, drawing inspiration from the dry textured surface. Made in white stoneware clay, parts are decorated with red and black iron oxide, and blue and orange stoneware glazes, and assembled after firing with the driftwood.

ABOVE: **Figure 114** Elizabeth Elston: *Red Driftwood.*

RIGHT: **Figure 115** Jo Connell: long pebble stack on driftwood.

Jo Connell's work reflects her love of the Isle of Wight coastline, where she gathers the driftwood used in her wall pieces. She makes press-moulded 'pebble' forms using coloured stoneware clays rolled and joined together in the agate-ware style.

Claire Ireland is always looking for 'found' objects that spark off ideas and, in this case (Figure 116), she found the

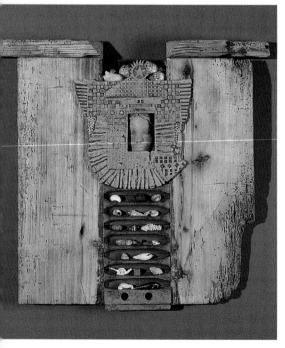

Figure 116 Claire Ireland: *Kangaroo in the Bush.* (Photo: Kit Young).

broomhead washed up on a Suffolk beach. The kangaroo developed in her fertile imagination in response to it.

In this wall piece (Figure 117) Alasdair MacDonell has combined found wood, stones, shells, coral and bone with the stoneware-fired ceramics.

Mark Smith's recent work is about journeys, and he incorporates in it found objects that hold memories. Here (Figure 118) he has made a fanciful boat with a barium stoneware glaze that rests in a niche naturally occurring in the drift-wood stand.

Health and safety

Many woodworking tools are sharp and can be dangerous, and you will need to familiarise yourself with their correct usage. While any dust given off could itself be hazardous, some people may become allergic to the small particles of particular woods. The wearing of masks and goggles is advised when dusty jobs are being done, and an extraction system should be considered. Wear a full mask when working on a lathe.

LEFT: **Figure 117** Alasdair MacDonell: *The Collector*, height 48cm (19in.). (Photo: Alasdair MacDonell)

OPPOSITE: **Figure 118** Mark Smith: *Boat.*

Chapter 8

Gallery of sculptural approaches

Peter Hayes is not limited by the rules of making – in fact, he likes to push technical boundaries and perceptions of what is possible. He makes large-scale ceramic forms that are placed in the landscape, and smaller pieces for domestic settings. He has travelled extensively and is touched by the ability of village potters to make 'exquisitely beautiful' vessels with simple tools and few facilities.

He makes in an individual way, throwing slabs of clay onto wooden boards that are covered with dry clay fragments and oxides; they are stretched and pounded by the process, which is repeated until the whole clay body and surface has taken on a character and texture that could only have been made in this way.

He works with a variety of clays, which have their own character, but often chooses a smooth clay that he encourages to crack under the thermal shock of the raku process by spraying with cold water. He then reassembles the shards, joining them with epoxy resin coloured with powder paints; this enhances and emphasises the joins.

Minerals, such as iron and copper, are introduced into the ceramic surface and these alter and develop with the effects of the elements over time. This process is speeded up with smaller pieces by covering the surface with wallpaper

OPPOSITE: **Figure 119** Peter Hayes: *Raku Bow with Blue Wave.*

paste to which the iron and copper is added. These are then submerged into the sea or the river outside his studio for a few months, identified by long strings tied to each so that he does not loose them. The iron and copper salts seep into the clay surface, which is dried and polished to give a feel and look of old leather.

Hayes and his family put on a good show at potters' markets, controlling the danger of raku firing but exploiting the drama to excite onlookers. Recently he has made a 3m (10ft) living water sculpture, which he takes to shows. Water is pumped to the top of the sculpture and allowed to run down the outside before re-circulating. The continually wet, textured surface is the ideal environment for seeds to germinate and is a good talking point.

Emma Rodgers uses 'film, photography and drawing' to research the way animals and humans move; in particular she is interested in examining, in detail, the bone structure and muscle formations of animals and humans in movement. A jagged line in a drawing is reinterpreted as a torn clay edge, and a soft pencil line might become a rolled clay form. She stretches and tears the clay to the point at which it splits and breaks so a 'split edge becomes a shoulder blade or a rusty nail becomes a jaw bone'.

She uses whatever materials she needs to make a piece work and includes different clay bodies, steel, perspex, found objects, fabrics, resin, wax and

occasionally gold leaf. She also has some of her pieces cast in bronze.

The work is built from a variety of white clays and porcelain, and grows by joining together torn 'patties and brandy snaps'. She does not usually use a wire armature but sometimes uses pieces of wire or found nails to act as a 'drawn' line. After bisque firing to 1140°C (2084°F) it is painted with a watery solution of underglaze or manganese dioxide, using large soft brushes. She applies monoprints made with black earthenware glaze in specific areas to represent the lines in her drawings. The work is re-fired to 1140°C (2084°F) with a soak, and then smoke-fired in magazine pages, straw and sawdust. The magazine pages give subtle hues from the coloured printing ink and the sawdust provides the soft greys.

In this work (Figure 120), Rodgers explores the reconstruction of shards and fragments found on archaeological sites, where the missing pieces are not 'filled in', but an adjustable armature holds the shards in their correct positions in relation to the complete sculptured figure, leaving the onlooker to visualise the whole. She uses steel rods held in place with bolts onto a central upright, which are positioned during the making process. The ceramic fragments and sections are attached to the steel structure by means of holes that are 10% bigger to allow for shrinkage. The fragments are fired and the armature adjusted to allow for the shrinkage, and then reassembled.

Nikki Pugh is interested in the contrast between the sensuous, burnished surfaces of tiny smoke-fired vessels and the hard-edged, engineered qualities of aluminium and the rubber components that make

the rims, hinges and lids to seal them. Often the balance of the handheld vessel changes as stoppers are removed or hinges lifted, each vessel having its own personality and patterns of behaviour.

These sculptural vessel forms are built from porcelain using a combination of press moulding and coiling techniques, which are then beaten, scraped and burnished at different stages as they dry. She likes to leave traces of the method of production evidenced by the finger indentation left on the interior surface and the burnishing marks on the exterior. A low bisque firing (800°C/1472°F) is followed by a sawdust firing and the surface sealed with beeswax polish.

Pugh did a degree in Metallurgy and Materials Engineering before embarking on an art-based degree and has found she is bringing together knowledge and experience gleaned from both courses.

Figure 122 Tod Shanafelt: *Shelf Problem.*

Aluminium fittings are designed for each vessel, taking into account such factors as shape of opening, patterns resulting from the sawdust firing and the overall shape of the vessel. Components are produced using a combination of silversmithing techniques and engineering processes.

Static components are fixed in position using two-part epoxy glue, while moveable components usually include rubber 'washers' at the metal/ceramic interface. Rubber is also utilised as a tensioning device to hold components in position.

Tod Shanafelt's work refers to the way memory alters, enhances and mystifies the past. Domestic in scale, it makes reference to tools, devices and components in his father's engineering workshop that, when he was a child,

seemed to hold meaning, knowledge and importance beyond his understanding, but that he associates with a feeling of love and respect for his father.

He scours thrift shops, scrapyards and recycling centres for found artefacts, which he assembles with handcrafted components in a variety of materials. Sometimes he uses French titles or words within the piece, hinting at knowledge and meanings that tantalise us, leaving us wanting to know more. His sculptures look as if they may have had a function in a previous life, but as this function is not known or is misunderstood, they become shrines with unknown histories.

The lime green and black wheel-thrown and assembled pieces (Figure 122) are fired to 1170°C (2138°F). He uses commercial decals and displays them on a painted steel wall-hung shelf to complete the industrial atmosphere of

Figure 123 Alasdair MacDonell: Untitled, private collection, Taiwan.

the whole assemblage.

Alasdair MacDonell is interested in the way the history of a piece is evident in its surface and form. More recently, he has been using found objects within his finished work. He has combined stoneware, wood, pewter, shells, stones and a seedpod into this wall piece (Figure 123).

His work reflects his interest in making personal relics of particular places and events, which are stimulated by collecting rubbish and waste. Clay has the ability to mimic other materials and, initially, the found objects were cast in plaster and used to make clay surfaces and textures, but in recent years some of the actual source materials have begun to appear with the glazed clay as part of the finished

Figure 124 Stuart Smith: *Behind the Oberoi.* (Photo: Jan Smith)

pieces. Currently he uses wood, copper and pewter foil, stones, shells, seeds, pods, wire, nails, mesh fabric, leather, hair and sheet steel. The found objects display strong evidence of history and experience, whether it be the erosion of the sea and wind, the patterns of burrowing insects or the marks of nails and fixings from a previous life – they speak of time,

damage and unknown relationships.

Stuart Smith has all the engineering skills required by a model maker and works successfully in a variety of materials. The realism of his raku-fired Indian figures is amazing. He uses white stoneware paperclay and models his pieces hollow using a wooden armature or supports. These are designed to be

Figure 125 Claire Ireland: *The Bird Tamer.*

taken away when the form is hardened enough to support itself. All the pieces are bisque fired to 1150°C (2102°F) then coloured with underglazes and low-firing alkaline glaze. He raku fires to 1000°C (1832°F) and then covers with damp sawdust to 'alter' the colours and surface quality. They are allowed to cool naturally, as to quench them in water would cause too much thermal shock.

He combines realistic metal and fibreglass accessories for his figures; one might have a bicycle and another an umbrella. The tyres of the bike are press-moulded and he uses copper tubing, stainless steel, iron rod, washers, nuts and bolts to fabricate the rest of the bike, which is made to scale. The

ABOVE: **Figure 126** Emili Biarnes Raber: *Arch* 55 × 20cm (22 × 8in.).

OPPOSITE: **Figure 127** Sally MacDonell: *Mother and Baby*, ht: 48cm (19in.). (Photo: Ron Sloman)

umbrella is made from fibreglass and parts of a dismantled full-size umbrella.

Claire Ireland is fascinated by the tribal and ceremonial aspects of past cultures and their ritual objects, which intrigue and mystify. This cheerful, narrative piece (Figure 125) brings together ceramics, copper, wood, twigs, seaweed and a sea-weathered brick. The ceramic elements are made from T-material and fired from between 1100°C (2012°F) and 1260°C (2300°F) with texture, colour and glaze dependent on the piece. Where necessary, holes are made in the ceramic parts when leather-hard to enable assembly after firing. She suggests stories by the use of titles and by the way disparate elements are bought together, but leaves the onlooker to bring their own interpretation.

Lustreware has a history in Spain dating back to the Moorish invasion of the Middle Ages. Raber's modern influences are many, but he particularly mentions Hans Coper, Claudi Casanovas and the illustrator Moebius. He considers the piece as a whole, not wanting any material or process to dominate. He sometimes uses parts of old agricultural implements that he finds in the countryside, bringing with them hints of their former history.

Figure 126 shows a sculptural platter supported by a tiny foot and is a wonderful example of his work with metallic lustres created by reduction firing alkaline glazes with metallic salts and oxides. The iron fragments are fired with the piece and are bonded to the clay by the oxidisation of the metal surface.

Sally MacDonell makes smoke-fired female figures with exotic headdresses, inspired by African sculpture. She hand-builds with torn slabs and 'brandy snap'

Figure 128 Julie Miles: *Don't Eat The Daisies.*

sections, using porcelain for its purity, and bisque fires to 1040°C (1904°F). After the bisque firing she applies washes of copper oxide and paints with a white engobe. The figures are then fired to 1170°C (2138°F) before smoke firing in sawdust to give subtle browns that are controlled to some extent by masking with tape and slip. She adds small sections of thin pewter sheet, which she patinates to suggest adornment and to draw attention to a gesture.

Julie Miles usually makes small, framed, wall-hung domestic pieces, but when challenged to make a larger piece for a garden sculpture competition, produced this exciting piece (Figure 128). She makes ceramic 'fossils' that refer to the 'fragility of nature' by dipping marigolds into porcelain slip, which she puts in the kiln when wet and high fires to 1300°C (2372°F). In this piece she has attached them to copper stems with an 'engineering bond' held in place by a neat ceramic collar. She chose copper for the stems as they will go green over time. They are driven into the ground for outdoor use, and into a block of oak or other hard-wood for more flexible positioning.

Suppliers

UK Ceramic Suppliers

Bath Potter's Supplies
Unit 18, Forth Avenue,
Westfield Trading Estate,
Radstock, BA3 4XE
Tel 01761 411077
www.bathpotters.demon.co.uk

Briar Wheels and Suppliers Ltd
Whitsbury Road, Fordingbridge,
Hants, SP 1NQ
Tel 01425 652991
www.briarwheels.co.uk

Brick House Ceramic Supplies
The Barn, Sheepcotes Lane,
Silver End, Witham,
Essex, CM8 3PJ
Tel 01376 585655

Potclays Ltd
Brick Kiln Lane, Etruria,
Stoke-on-Trent, Staffs, ST4 7B
Tel 01782 219816

Potterycrafts Ltd
Campbell Road, Stoke-on-Trent,
Staffs, ST4 4ET
Tel 01782 745000
www.potterycrafts.co.uk

UK Kiln Suppliers

Cromartie Ltd
Park Hall Road, Longton,
Stoke-on-Trent, Staffs, ST3 5AY
Tel 01782 319435

Kiln and Furnaces
Keele Street Works, Tunstall
Stoke-on-Trent,
Staffs, ST6 5AS
Tel 01782 813621

Laser Kilns Ltd
1 Coopersdale Road,
London, E9 6AY

UK Mould Suppliers

Specialist Refractory Services Ltd
Amber Business Centre
Riddings near Alfreton,
Derby, DE55 4BR

UK Silicone Rubber

Ambersil
Whiting Road, Basingstoke
Hants, RG24 0WS

Dow Corning Hansil Ltd
19 Wintersells Road, Byfleet
Surrey, KT14 7LH
Tel 01932 351911

European Glass Suppliers

A.Pfann
Naarderstraat 73–75
1211 AK Hilversum
Netherlands

Plowden & Thompson Ltd
Dial Glassworks, Stourbridge
West Midlands, DY8 4YN
England
Tel: 01384 393398

Schott Glass Ltd
Aston Fields Industrial Estate
Drummond Road, Stafford, ST16 3EL
England
Tel: 01785 223166
www.schott.com/uk/english

Schott-Weisenthathutte GMbH
D7070 Schwabisch Gmund,
Perenweg 3, Postfach 1169
Germany

Zimmermann Color Glass
PO Box 6, D-87656 Germaringen
Germany
Tel: (849) 83 41 65 22 1
www.colorglasszimmermann.com

UK Precious Metal & Metal Leaf Suppliers

Betts Metal Sales Ltd
  49–63 Spencer Street
  Hockley, Birmingham B18 6DE
  England
  Tel: 0121 233 2413
  www.bettsmetals.co.uk

Cooksons Precious Metals Ltd
  59-83 Vittoria Stteet
  Birmingham B1 8NZ, England
  Tel: 0121 2002120
  www.cooksongold.com

Habberley Meadows
Gold Leaf Manufacturers
  5 Saxon Way, Chelmsley Wood
  Birmingham, B37 5Y
  Tel: 0121 770 0103
  www.habberleymeadows.co.uk

E. Ploton (Sundries) Ltd
  Guilding Materials
  273 Archway Road
  London N6 5AA
  Tel: 0208 348 0315
  www.ploton.co.uk

Silver Alchemy Supplies
  2 Marshall Street,
  London W1F 9BB
  Tel: 08707 517 607
  www.silveralchemy.com

UK Wire Suppliers

[*Ferrous and non-ferrous metal wire*]
Fays Metals Ltd
  Unit 1, 37 Colville Road
  Alton, W3 8BL

[*Dental steel wire*]
Scientific Wire Co.
  18 Raven Road
  London, E18 8HW
  www.scientificwire.com

[*Copper and silver wire*]
Stephen Simpson Ltd
  Avenham Road Works
  Preston, Lancashire,
  PR1 3UH

UK Jewellery Suppliers

Cookson and Exchange Findings
  49 Hatton Garden, The City
  London, EC1N 8YS
  Tel 0207400 6500

Cousins Tool Centre
  41 Warstone Lane, Hockley
  Birmingham, B18 6JJ
  Tel +44 (0)121 237 5600

Slimbrand
Precision Products in Precious Metals
  65-66 Warstone Lane, Hockley
  Birmingham, B18 6NG
  Tel 0121 212 2560
  www.slimbrand.co.uk

TH Findings Ltd
  42 Hylton Street, Hockley
  Birmingham, B18 6HN
  Tel 0121 554 9889
  www.thfindings.com

UK Electrical Suppliers

Collingwood VLM
  Brooklands House, Sywell Aerodrome
  Sywell, Northampton, NN6 0BT
  Tel 01604 495151
  www.collingwoodgroup.com

[*Luminescent Panels*]
Glow Safe Ltd
  126 Hallen Road, Henbury
  Bristol, BS10 7RB
  Tel: 08701 998524
  www.glow-safe-com

Specialist Lamp Fitting Supplies
  17 Acton Avenue, Appleton
  Warrington, Cheshire, WA4 5PS
  Tel 01925 604314
  www.specialistlampfittingsupplies.co.uk

UK Textile Suppliers

Fibrecrafts
  Old Portsmouth Road, Peasmarsh
  Guildford, GU3 1LZ
  Tel: 01483 565800
  www.fibrecrafts.com

Rainbow Silks
6 Wheelers Yard, High Street
Great Missenden,
Buckinghamshire, HP16 0AL
www.rainbowsilks.co.uk

Whaleys (Bradford) Ltd
Harris Court, Great Horton
Bradford, W. Yorkshire, BD7 4EQ
Tel: 01274 576718
www.whaleys-bradford.ltd.uk/contact.cfm

Wingham Wool Work
Freepost, 70 Main Street
Wentworth, S. Yorkshire, S62 7BR
Tel: 01226 742926
www.winghamwoolwork.co.uk

North American Ceramic Suppliers

American Art Clay Company
4717 W.16th Street,
Indianapolis, IN 46222,
Tel: (800)374-1600 /(317) 244-6871
www.amaco.com

A.R.T Studio Clay Company
9320 Michigan Avenue,
Sturterant, WI 53177-2425,
Tel: (262) 884-4278
www.artclay.com

Axner Pottery Supply
PO Box 621484,
Oviedo, FL 32762-1484, Freephone
800-843-7057/407-365-2600
www.axner.com

Continental Clay Company
1101 Stintson Blvd,
N.E. Minneapolis, MN 55413
Tel (800) 432 CLAY
www.continentalclay.com

Davens
5076, Peachtree Road, Atlanta
Georgia, 30341,
Tel (770) 451-2105
www.davensceramiccenter.com

Duncan Ceramics Products Inc.
5673 E. Shields Ave., Fresno,
California, 93727
Tel (800 237-2642)/(559) 2914444

Laguna Clay Company
14400 Lomitas Avenue,
City of Industry, CA 91746
Tel: (800) 452-4862
www.lagunaclay.com

Mile Hi Ceramics,
77 Lipan, Denver, Colorado,
80223-1580
Tel: (303) 825-4570
www.milehiceramics.com

Minnesota Clay Co.
Normandale Tech.Centre,
Bloomington, MN 55439
Tel (952) 884-9104
www.mm.com/mnclayus

The Potter's Shop
31 Thorpe Road, Needham,
Massachusettes, MA 02194
Tel: (017) 449-7687
www.thepottersshop.com

Tucker's Pottery Supplies Inc.,
Unit 7, 15 West Pearce Street,
Richmond Hill,
Ontario, Canada L4B 1H6
Tel: 1 905 889-7705
www.tuckerspottery.com

USA Glass Suppliers

Bullseye Glass Co.
3722 SE 21st Avenue
Portland, Oregan 97202, USA
www.bullseyeglass.com

Franciscan Glass Co. Inc
100 San Antonio Circle,
Mountain View,
California 94040, USA

Hollander Glass Co.
140 58th Street, Brooklyn
New York NY11220, USA

SA Bendheim Co. Inc
61 Willet Street
Bassaic NJ 07055, USA

Spectrum Glass Co. Inc
PO Box 646, Woodsville
Washington 98072, USA
www.spectrumglass.com

Bibliography

Ceramics

Barley, N. *Smashing Pots, Feats of Clay from Africa*, British Museum Press, 1994

Bennett, P. 'Putting in the boot', *Ceramic Review*, May/June, 1997

Birks, T. *Pottery – A Complete Guide to Pottery-making Techniques*, A & C Black, 1988

Birks, T. *Hans Coper* (revised edn), Marston House, 1991

Cooper, E. *A History of World Pottery*, BT Batsford Ltd, 1988

Daniel Clark Foundation, *The Studio Potter*, Daniel Clark Foundation, 1982

Salter, P. (compiler and editor), *300 Tonnes of Clay*, catalogue, University of Wolverhampton, 1996

The 'Ceramic Handbook' series, published by A & C Black

Precious metal clay

McCreight, T. *Working with Precious Metal Clay*, A & C Black, 2000

Metalwork/jewellery techniques

Hughes, R. and Rowe, M. *The Colouring, Bronzing and Patination of Metals*, Crafts Council, 1982

McCreight, T. *Jewellery: Fundamentals of Metalsmithing*, (Jewellery S), A & C Black, 1998

McGrath, J. *Basic Jewellery Making*, Quantum Books Ltd, 1997

McGrath, J. *The Encyclopaedia of Jewelry-Making Techniques*, Running Press Book Publishers, 2003

Utracht, O. *Metalwork Techniques for Craftsmen*, Robert Hale, 1974

Wicks, S. *The Jewellery Making Manual*, McDonalds Press, 1985

Textiles

Dean, J. *Wild Colour*, Mitchell Beazley, 1999

Kinnersly-Taylor, J. *Dyeing and Screenprinting on Textiles*, (Printmaking Handbook), A & C Black, 2003

Scott, J. *Textiles Perspectives in Mixed Media Sculpture*, Crowood Press, 2003

Terry, T. *Handmade Bags (Textiles)*, A & C Black, 2002

Wells, K. *Fabric Dyeing and Printing*, Conran Octopus, 2000

Sculpture

Acero, R. *Making Ceramics Sculpture, Techniques, Projects and Inspirations*, Lark Books, 2001

Butler, V. *Casting for Sculptors*, A & C Black, 1997

Plowman, J. *Manual of Sculpture Techniques*, A & C Black, 2003

Glass

Bray, C. *A Dictionary of Glass*, A & C Black, 2001

Cummings, K. *Techniques of Kiln-formed Glass*, A & C Black, 1997

Eberle, B. *Creative Glass Techniques*, A & C Black, 2001

Metal Leaf

Fielding, A. 'Bristling with energy', *Ceramic Review* 181, Jan/Feb, 2000

Sloan, A. *Decorative Gilding*, Collins & Brown Ltd, 1996

Wood

Andrews, J. *The Sculpture of David Nash*, Lund Humphries, 2001

Glossary

Anneal To heat materials and allow to cool slowly, in order to remove internal stresses. Metal needs to be annealed regularly during forming to make it malleable. Glass needs to be annealed during firing otherwise it is likely to crack.

Borax A flux used by jewellers which comes in a solid cone and, when ground with water, forms a milky consistency, used to aid soldering.

Ball plein hammer General metalwork hammer with one ball-shaped end.

Carve To shape a piece of solid material, like wood or plaster, with chisels.

Cast A way to duplicate objects by pouring either molten or liquid materials into a mould.

Crucible Receptacle into which metals may be melted.

Dye A natural or synthetic substance used to add colour or change the colour of something.

Felt A fabric made by rolling and pressing wool until the fibres become matted.

Float glass Sheet glass which is cast onto a bed of molten tin.

Forge To shape metal by heating in a fire or furnace, and beating or hammering.

Fusing Joining together separate glass elements by heating in a kiln to soften (usually 750–800°C/1382–1472°F).

Glass A brittle, usually transparent, material made by fusing together sand, soda, lime and sometimes other ingredients.

Gold size An organic glue used when applying metal leaf.

Horticultural glass Glass rolled into sheets suitable for greenhouses.

Iron binding wire Soft wire used to hold together metal sections when soldering.

Lead-free pewter Grey alloy including tin and copper.

Lost wax casting Wax models are made from a rubber mould made from an original metal component. During the lost wax technique molten metal replaces the wax which melts away to leave the metal replica of the wax model which needs to be filed and polished.

Metal leaf Fine sheets of precious and other metals applied for decorative purposes.

Patinate To alter the colour of a metal by oxidisation with chemicals or heat.

Pallion Tiny square of silver solder.

Pendant motor Portable rotating motor which hangs above the jeweller and takes different jewellery tools for polishing, drilling, texturing etc.

Pickle Dilute sulphuric acid which is used to clean metal after soldering.

Piercing saw Type of fine saw used by jewellers with disposable blades of different grades.

Rouge Greasy polish used with a pendant motor or polisher when polishing jewellery.

Spot-weld Fuse together metal by heat.

Silver solder Silver alloy which, when heated with borax, melts and joins together two pieces of metal.

Slumping Bending glass, within the kiln, over or into a mould.

Silicone rubber A flexible synthetic substance used to make moulds for casting low melt metal alloys.

Solder To join together two or more pieces of metal with use of borax flux and pallions of solder with heat administered equally to each piece.

Tin snips Cutters similar to scissors used for rough cutting of sheet metal.

Torch Jewellers blow torch can be used with either mains or propane gas cylinder.

Turn To shape wood, attached to the rotating face of a lathe, with chisels.

Weave To form a fabric by interlacing long threads with others at right angles to them.

Index